The Frog Run

THE *CREDO* SERIES

A *credo* is a statement of belief, an assertion of deep conviction. The *Credo* series offers contemporary American writers whose work emphasizes the natural world and the human community the opportunity to discuss their essential goals, concerns, and practices. Each volume presents an individual writer's *credo,* his or her investigation of what it means to write about human experience and society in the context of the more-than-human world, as well as a biographical profile and complete bibliography of the author's published work. The *Credo* series offers some of our best writers an opportunity to speak to the fluid and subtle issues of rapidly changing technology, social structure, and environmental conditions.

The Frog Run

Words and Wildness in the Vermont Woods

John Elder

Scott Slovic, *Credo* Series Editor

Credo

MILKWEED EDITIONS

Published 2001 by Milkweed Editions
Printed in Canada
Cover photo courtesy of the author
Back cover photo courtesy of Scott Slovic
Cover design by Dale Cooney
The text of this book is set in Stone Serif.
01 02 03 04 05   5 4 3 2 1
First Edition

Milkweed Editions, a nonprofit publisher, gratefully acknowledges support from our World As Home funders: Lila-Wallace Reader's Digest Fund, and Reader's Legacy underwriter Elly Sturgis. Other support has been provided by the Elmer L. and Eleanor J. Andersen Foundation; Bush Foundation; Faegre and Benson Foundation; General Mills Foundation; Marshall Field's Project Imagine with support from the Target Foundation; McKnight Foundation; Minnesota State Arts Board through an appropriation by the Minnesota State Legislature and a grant from the National Endowment for the Arts, and a grant from the Wells Fargo Foundation Minnesota; A Resource for Change technology grant from the National Endowment for the Arts; Lawrence and Elizabeth Ann O'Shaughnessy Charitable Income Trust in honor of Lawrence M. O'Shaughnessy; Oswald Family Foundation; Ritz Foundation on behalf of Mr. and Mrs. E. J. Phelps Jr.; John and Beverly Rollwagen Fund of the Minneapolis Foundation; St. Paul Companies, Inc.; Star Tribune Foundation; Target Stores; U.S. Bancorp Piper Jaffray Foundation; and generous individuals.

Library of Congress Cataloging-in-Publication Data

Elder, John, 1947–
  The frog run : words and wildness in the Vermont woods / John Elder.— 1st ed.
      p.   cm. — (Credo)
  Includes bibliographical references.
  ISBN 1-57131-258-7 (pbk. : acid-free paper)
  1. Natural history—Vermont.   2. Elder, John, 1947–   3. Go
(Game)   4. Christianity.   5. Maple syrup.   I. Title.   II. Credo series
(Minneapolis, Minn.)

QH105.V7 E43 2002
508.743—dc21

                                                              2001042736

This book is printed on acid-free, recycled paper.

To Gary Snyder,
whose writings and example
have been such an inspiration.
Sensei: *the one who goes before.*

The Frog Run

The Frog Run

The Frog Run

WORDS AND WILDNESS IN THE
VERMONT WOODS

by John Elder

Prologue

Boiling down the sap of sugar maples to produce
syrup traditionally occupies Vermont farmers from
about the end of February each year. March and April
are mud season in the Green Mountains. The melt-
ing of four months of snow makes rivers rage, and
fields get too mucky for walking, much less for driving a tractor or a team of animals. But this time is
also when life rekindles in the maples that dominate
our forests, from the mountains' middle elevations
down into the valleys. The sap of sugar maples is
twice as rich in sugars as that of most deciduous trees.
The Abenaki people discovered thousands of years
ago that, if concentrated, it yielded a delicious natural sweetener. They produced it by sliding stones that
had been heated to a glow into large birch-bark containers of sap, adding new stones to keep it at a
boil. Yankee farmers who learned this art from the
Abenaki developed their own evaporators—flat pans
simmering above a wood-fired arch of bricks. But

3

the goal was identical—to condense watery sap to syrup.

Because the early settlers in Vermont often lived in such isolation, this product meant much more to them than the delicacy we pour on our waffles. Throughout the nineteenth century, it was in fact common to transfer the finished syrup to a smaller, separate evaporator, where it could be reduced to granular maple sugar in a process known as "sugaring off." This allowed farmers to avoid the expense of imported cane sweeteners and, in years when they had extra to sell, provided an important cash supplement. Such a history explains why, even today, when syrup is in most cases the final product, variants of the more elemental word *sugar* define every aspect of the process. Sugaring takes the sap from a maple grove, or sugar bush, and renders it into syrup over an evaporator that steams beneath the opened roof-louvers of a sugarhouse. When March blizzards arrive, some of the syrup is boiled to an extra-thick state and then whipped up into the traditional confection called "sugar on snow."

Sap courses through the trees when the temperature rises above freezing during the day but drops below it at night. Sugarmakers can be ready for this tidal surge if they watch the ground. The remaining snow cover in the woods, smoothed out and shining from the late season slump that levels all, will begin to draw back in a circle around each maple's trunk. Longer days and stronger light warm the gray-brown bark and gradually create little wells that reach down until they touch the mud. You wouldn't want to set your taps much before these circles appear, since holes drilled in the trees fill back in and block the flow within a couple of months. On the other hand, it's important to be ready for the first good run of sap. There may only be three or four big runs in a year.

Sugarmakers thus pay keen attention to the fluctuations of temperatures and sap marking the year's passage from winter to spring. In February 2000 our own family began sugaring. Experiencing it for myself has helped me understand how important this annual project must have been, psychologically as well as economically, for the inhabitants of remote hill farms. Summer, fall, and winter in Vermont are glorious. Their essences are distilled, their contrasts dramatic. But spring always seems late and short. Weeks pass when winter has lost its grip but nothing new has taken its place. Watching the temperatures' courtly dance around the freezing line suddenly becomes exciting, however, when maple syrup is the culmination. Thoreau writes in *Walden:* "We should be blessed if we lived in the present always, and took advantage of every accident that befell us, like the grass which confesses the influence of the slightest dew that falls on it; and did not spend our time in atoning for the neglect of past opportunities, which we call doing our duty. We loiter in winter while it is already spring." Amid the half-frozen, half-sodden fields and the late snowstorms, the pulse of sap turns us toward the present's wavering shore.

Not only does sugaring help us remember that

spring is coming, it also gives us a reason for desiring that it not progress any *faster*. Once we have awakened to it, we long to dwell in this protracted in-between. This time for standing in the warm, sticky sugarhouse, witnessing the alchemy of air and water into gold. For talking through the night with family beside the simmering evaporator. Or for drinking a beer with friends who step into the sugarhouse and out of their usual routines. We want this time, once the sap is running and the sugarwood is in and the evaporator is all fired up, to last forever. But no season does—even, or especially, when it's one we've decided, after some reservations, to celebrate.

Sometimes a last run of sap will carry sugaring into late April. This is the sugarmaker's equivalent of spring skiing, compounding the pleasures of two seasons into one. But such fantasy moments are short-lived, as the peepers remind us. One effect of snow-melt is the appearance of vernal pools in little swales amid the hills, or in low meadows along the highways where water may for a brief time stand several feet deep. Salamanders and frogs breed in these pools that contain no fish to devour their eggs. As the festival of generation commences, several species of small frogs suddenly fill the nights with their choruses. The burden of their refrain—maybe of most refrains—is "Love! Now! Quick!"

Such singing keeps the ebullience of the season well stoked. But once the peepers have tuned up, the old-timers say that there will be just one more week of good boiling in the sugarhouse. Such vernal music seems to coincide with a swelling of the maple buds, from which, in turn, the sap will take on a funky taste. This new tinge of flavor would be distilled and intensified in the process of reducing forty gallons of sap to one of syrup, and would end up doing little to enhance a stack of pancakes. The final week of a late sugaring season, when musical excitement fills the nights and there is still untainted sap to boil down, is thus referred to, in a phrase at once celebratory and elegiac, as "the frog run."

That phrase captures for me the ludicrous urgency of the peepers' moment—and the human moment, too. It expresses the fact that we must soon relinquish this harvest we have only recently learned to claim. Focusing all the more intensely on the process as it nears its end, we remember the softening snow that signaled its onset and anticipate the cleanup and the battening down of the sugarhouse for another year. The three essays that follow are my own frog run, like a year's last jugs of syrup, carrying the harvest of one season into the untapped morning of whatever comes next.

They coincide both with our family's completion of a first season of sugaring and with my conclusion of a twenty-seventh year teaching at Middlebury College. When we moved to Vermont right after graduate school, my wife, Rita, and I never anticipated that we would end up sinking our roots and raising our children so far from our parents and brothers in the San Francisco Bay Area. But as the years passed, we came to realize that, here in the Green Mountains, we had found our true place on earth. We will never leave Vermont.

Staying put does not mean that the world slows down around us, though. If anything, being grounded lends vividness and velocity to the circling seasons and makes us more keenly aware of generational transitions in our family or village. This invitation to write about "goals, concerns, and practices" for the *Credo* series feels like a good chance to explore the continuities of my life and work at a time of such transitions.

The first essay in this collection offers a vision of wilderness and sustainability in my adopted state, while the second chronicles my evolution as a reader. The third relates our family's adventure in sugaring and reflects upon the ways it helps us belong more deeply to Vermont. As disparate as these topics might sound, they feel to me like variations on the theme of coalescence, and also register a similar sense of urgency. As the dialogue about the future of wilderness in Vermont rises to a new intensity, as I move into my final chapter of teaching at Middlebury, and as the youngest of our three children starts college, I hear a singing in the air that announces the frog run. Sap's flowing strongly, but we won't keep boiling for too much longer this season. Open the louvers and fire up the evaporator. Sleeping can wait until next week.

Aji

On a clear morning at the beginning of July, I drive south on Forest Road 49 in the Green Mountain National Forest. The narrow track skirts Boyden Brook, first on the east side and then, after a zigzag that takes me across a rudimentary bridge, on the west. I park at a locked gate, near which a party of teenagers is sleeping in, on, and beside several cars. They lie there in the ludicrous beauty of adolescence, hair tangled and sweatshirts wadded up as makeshift pillows. Their pale faces are scrunched up against the dawn that illuminates them like a spotlight. But all seem deeply asleep, without the slightest twitch or sharp intake of breath when this stranger walks past them into the woods—as if they are entranced, waiting for the next scene in *A Midsummer Night's Dream* to begin.

I continue along an old logging road until it meets another fork of the brook. Grasses crowd the muddy roadsides, their seed heads ripe and drooping. Oxeye daisies, yellow jewelweed, and purple flowering raspberry all flourish here, too, along with the tall nettles that will begin going to seed at the end of the month and establish way stations for the goldfinches. Now's when I start bushwhacking up the slope to my south—passing through some patchcuts from several years back in which the red-berried elder are in their prime, with elongated clusters of berries bending down the terminal twigs.

The colors brightening my hike mark the early stage of a successional process. These are tendrils of the forest, repossessing the light-filled clearings of road and patch-cuts. Such a process advances quickly in our wet Vermont landscape. If the logging road were to be abandoned altogether, it would soon turn into a goldenrod and steeplebush thicket—as so many abandoned meadows in this formerly agricultural stretch of the Green Mountains have already done. Then might follow a stand of staghorn sumac, with the crimson of their compound, spear-shaped leaves brilliant for a few falls before the pines and maples push them out in their turn. Eventually, only a few, more muted flowers, like bunchberry at the season's beginning and whorled wood aster near its end, will be left to bloom in the filtered light of a resurgent forest.

Robert Frost, who owned a farm just on the other side of Route 125, described the process of reforestation in these stanzas from "Something for Hope":

> At the present rate it must come to pass,
> And that right soon, that the meadowsweet
> And steeple bush, not good to eat,
> Will have crowded out the edible grass.
>
> Then all there is to do is wait
> For maple, birch, and spruce to push
> Through meadowsweet and steeple bush
> And crowd them out at a similar rate.

His speaker seems to be consoling a farmer who is discouraged about the disappearance of tilled fields in northern New England. Frost's poem offers a vision of succession within which farms and forests, human loss and gain, are all part of a comprehensive cycle. This morning, as I hike up into a portion of the Green Mountain National Forest that has recently been proposed as a new wilderness area, I feel grateful for such an inclusive, and ironic, perspective. It affirms the forest's persistence in this long-settled but beautiful landscape, and makes it possible to think about wilderness in the future tense, not just in the present and past.

I continue to pass through sunny openings amid the trees, even after leaving those roadside patch-cuts behind. These are stands of beech and birch that show the dramatic effects of an ice storm in the winter of '98. At certain elevations in the Green Mountains—often, it seems, between one thousand and two thousand feet—it looks as if a heavy chain was dragged through the treetops. Trunks up to a foot in diameter were snapped off by the weight of thickly coating ice. The woods above our village of Bristol sounded as if they were enduring an aerial bombardment in that ice storm. Explosive bursts followed by reverberant crashes continued through the windless night. I notice that many of these broken trees are now producing healthy foliage on their remaining branches. Often, too, thick new bunches of leaves seem to grow right out of the trunk, just below the break. They match the bright green of herbaceous plants around me on the forest floor, seizing their own chance to prosper in these post-storm clearings.

Climbing past the wreckage of the ice storm, I am

approaching a much more ancient and long-lasting perturbation of the forest's main flow. The central ridge of the Green Mountains runs north-south for most of the length of Vermont, in an extension of the larger Appalachian thrust. But just ahead of me is a line of peaks nearly perpendicular to it. Philadelphia Peak, Monastery Mountain, and Worth Mountain run from east to west before joining the central spine near Romance Mountain, the other three-thousand-footer in the vicinity.

Such a rampart wedged against the topographic grain has had the effect of thwarting road builders in a large segment of the Green Mountain National Forest. Bounded on the west by Middlebury and Route 7 and on the east by Hancock and Route 100, it runs south from Bread Loaf and Route 125 all the way down to Rochester, Goshen, and Salisbury. Another large roadless area opens up again to the south of those towns. I continue climbing, leaving behind the evidence of the ice storm and far from any trail, until I move into a challenging terrain dominated by spruce and fir. They and paper birch thrive above twenty-two hundred feet or so in the Green Mountains. Along with their understory of hobblebush, mountain maple, and mountain ash, they make up the characteristic forest community of our ridgelines. As I come closer to Monastery Mountain, the trees grow more massive than I am used to seeing in Vermont, the undergrowth less dense. Such mighty columns, standing above a spacious but shadowy forest floor, make me think of Frost's wonderful description in the poem "Come In" of mature eastern woods as "the pillared dark."

This forest, with its remoteness from roads and other human activity, harbors one of Vermont's healthiest populations of black bears. They can venture down to the lower-slope beech groves when putting on fat for the winter, then return to their winter dens with some assurance of seclusion. It may also be that, when combined with the twenty-two-thousand-acre Bread Loaf Wilderness Area just north of Route 125, such heights will provide a more reliable haven for the catamounts that have begun passing through our region again. A viable population of those slit-eyed ghosts, watching us even when we may not spot them, would represent for me the truest definition of recovered wilderness in Vermont.

Another sunny morning, but this time I'm writing at home, legs crossed in our old green recliner and with a narrow-ruled legal pad resting on the Go board in my lap. The board, approximately eighteen inches square and three inches thick, looks hefty. But its fine-grained wood is really quite light, as well as being remarkably resonant to the slightest tap. When one of the black Go stones, made of slate, or one of the white clamshell ones is set down crisply on the board during play, it delivers a lively *tock*. For that matter, it's producing quite a nice *plunk, plunk* right now, as I bounce my pencil eraser on it. Nineteen lines are drawn across the board and nineteen more run lengthwise. They meet in 361 intersections—the knots of a square black net, stretched taut on the playing surface, through which glows the living circulation of the wood.

Go is an ancient game of strategy with which I became fascinated during a sabbatical in Japan. Players try to surround certain areas of the board, taking turns to place one stone at a time on an intersection. With so many intersections, the range of possible moves is much vaster than that offered by the sixty-four squares of a chessboard. Thus, at the beginning of a game, one can feel as if several more or less separate contests are going on in the different corners. Gradually, though, the scatters of stones join and coalesce into a comprehensive pattern. This is the phase of a game when one begins to find certain small groups of one color more or less surrounded by larger groups of the other color. Isolated and outnumbered, they seem to have forfeited any future. But as the tides of play swirl round and round the board, reinforcements may arrive for these outriders. Or sometimes the surrounding stones are themselves overtaken and cut off. This surprising potential for apparently dead stones to spring back to life and influence is referred to by Go players as *aji*, a Japanese word meaning "a lingering taste."

I love this game in which the mutual enclosures of black and white stones, set against the subtle patterns of the wood, create a design more intricate than either player's single intention. It feels like the principle of plenitude at work, introducing appropriate inhabitants to each niche of a fertile ecosystem and establishing a larger order that encompasses the individual agendas of every organism. *Aji* is an important factor in biological succession and in Go alike. Dominance shifts back and forth. Relics of old engagements germinate, suddenly looking forward as well as back. Such ebbs and flows within wholeness define, among other things, the surprising reemergence of wilderness from the cutover landscape of Vermont. While there might have seemed to be an opposition between nature and civilization, or even a total domination of one by the other, the possibility has remained all along for a larger balance to be reasserted. I find consolation in witnessing these tides of loss and recovery, both on the Go board and in the mountains around our family's home. They help me understand my own experiences as a teacher, writer, and family person, here at the cusp of my fifty-fourth year. I can begin to see the extent to which all my own plans have been provisional, with their fulfillment coming not in the ways I might have anticipated but rather through being gathered into a more comprehensive, if not quite accountable, swirl.

An incident last semester shed light on both the progression and the irresolution of my work. My friend Scott Sanders visited campus and spent a couple of hours in my office while I went off to teach a class. When I walked back in the door to go to lunch with him, he asked with some bafflement just how my books were arranged. I laugh about that excellent question whenever I have occasion to scan the shelves. Name the system—Dewey Decimal, Library of Congress, alphabetical, generic, sorting by color, or grading by size—and it would find no purchase in this conglomeration. Some books do stand in respectable rows, but as often they lean and rise in the tilted layers of geological deformation. Or they simply lie in piles that may be framed by the boxed-in shelves but also may be on top of them, or on the rug beside them. Each of those rows, tilts, and piles is a jumble in its own right, too. Looking up now to the shelf above my computer screen, I can scan the following titles (from right to left): *Nature's Economy* by Donald Worster, *John Clare's Poetry,* John Wesley Powell's *The Exploration of the Colorado River and Its Canyons, Ulysses,* and *Who Dies?* by Stephen Levine. Or I can walk over to the shelf beside my office door and inspect a stack that includes *The Roadside Geology of Alaska, Scar Vegas and Other Stories* by Tom Paine (a novelist who teaches at Middlebury), and *Robert Frost's Poetry.* I rotate one book near the top whose spine was turned to the wall so that I couldn't read it: *Epitaph for a Peach* by David Mas Masumoto.

This selection of books is obviously not random, though, despite the fact that its order may be somewhat haphazard. Even so small a sample as described above reflects an interest in the zone where literature and the natural world intersect. Surveying the shelves more systematically from end to end confirms such an impression, especially when one pays attention to the groups of books by particular authors that appear here and there. In the tall bookcase against the far wall are clusters by Scott Russell Sanders, Wendell

Berry, and Gary Snyder. Rick Bass and Terry Tempest Williams share the same shelf of another case. Here, in the two shelves beside my computer table, are collections of poetry by A. R. Ammons and Mary Oliver. There are also individual titles that pop up in multiple editions from shelf to shelf. Wordsworth's poetry, *Walden,* and Leopold's *A Sand County Almanac* are in this category. And mixed, or scrambled, in with the nature writing and poetry are novels by Eliot, Woolf, Lawrence, and Howard Frank Mosher, books on chaos, evolution, Japanese literature, Vermont history, and forest ecology.

Taken together, these shelves tell the story of an English teacher who has increasingly focused on nature writing and other forms of environmental literature, and who is attempting now both to broaden his cultural frame of reference and integrate his teaching more fully with science. That's me. These books also reveal that integration is far from achieved, that no clear model has been arrived at for shaping the disparate elements into a pattern. My shelves frame an impulse, not a design. In my teaching, family life, and religious practice I find a similar lack of consistency. Yet in those areas, too, I sense that something has been gathering toward clarity. At least it feels that way in retrospect.

Right after completing graduate school, I was hired by the Middlebury English Department with an understanding that one of my main responsibilities would be in the area of British modernism. I loved my opportunities to teach books like *The Rainbow* and *To the Lighthouse,* and offered such courses annually for ten years. But then my interests began to shift toward writers of nonfiction and poetry who had a special interest in the natural world. The new direction resulted in part from having lived in Vermont for that decade. While lacking the sublime wilderness of the western mountains, this state's interfolding of forests, villages, and farms brought experiences of natural beauty into my daily life. My fascination with this landscape was heightened by the surprising fact that, for over a century and a half, it has been recovering from early deforestation, in effect becoming wilder every year.

One reason I take a special interest in the history of Vermont is that it helps me make sense of my own life history. In both regards, good things have come in roundabout and unanticipated ways. Looking back over the half of my life that has been led in this state, I don't feel anything like the satisfaction of completing a long-held plan. What I do feel is gratitude, heightened by an element of surprise. A prime object of this gratitude is Middlebury College, which has allowed me to follow my growing inclination toward teaching the literature of nature, given me a split appointment in English and Environmental Studies, and supported my desire both to study Japanese here at the college and to travel to Kyoto with my family on a sabbatical. Such generosity has allowed my teaching here, like my writing, my family life, and my religious experience, to feel like a path.

In our family, Rita's and my happy absorption in

parenting three young children gave way first to participation in a group of five campers, as we all undertook expeditions together around the country and abroad. This chapter shifted with bewildering suddenness into a tumult of teenagers. Now, as all three of our kids are out of high school, we are moving into a new phase none of us quite has a fix on.

In my religious life, too, the only constant has been change. I look back with wistful admiration at the remarkable steadiness of my parents' relationship with their faith community. For their entire lives, both remained in the Southern Baptist Church of their youth, attending services and prayer meetings without fail, teaching classes, singing in the choir, supporting the church generously in financial ways. That church was a core influence in my life through high school. When I left for college, my own religious quest commenced and has continued to this day. Like many students of my generation, I became opposed to the Vietnam War. In Claremont, California, where I was attending Pomona College, the Quakers took the lead in witnessing against the war and supporting students who wanted to find a way to protest it. The combination of clear moral vision and gatherings where "leadings from the spirit" were spoken out of the deep silence moved and impressed me. I attended the Society of Friends meetings on and off through college and graduate school. By 1970, Rita and I had married. Her background is Italian Catholic, and she is as faithful to her tradition as my parents were to theirs. During the grad school years in New Haven, we liked attending both Mass and Meeting together. The liturgical richness of the Catholic service complemented the simplicity and silence of the Quakers.

When we came to Middlebury in 1973, we found a wonderful Friends community that met in a school near the college campus. We regularly attended those meetings as well as Catholic services together. I became deeply involved in the Quakers, even serving as Clerk of the Meeting for a time. When our kids were small, one of the defining features of our family was this happy mixture of religious traditions. We would tell people who asked that we were Quatholics. Just as I retained great affection and respect for my parents' Baptist faith even when my own search took me in other directions, so too I continue to love the Middlebury Friends Meeting and the remarkable individuals in it, even as my path has diverged from them.

About eight years ago, I began sitting at the newly founded Vermont Zen Center in Shelburne. As my interest in Gary Snyder's poetry led me to study Japanese and to explore the haiku tradition of Bashō, Zen also grew increasingly attractive to me. Quakerism itself played some part in this interest, since the simplicity of the forms, the sitting in the silence, and the association with sixties rethinking of prevailing social structures all resembled Zen, at least in its American manifestation. In part, I suppose my desire to pursue Zen Buddhism in this newly available center was a cultural or aesthetic impulse. I wanted a personal experience of this tradition whose literature spoke to me so powerfully. In addition, though, I was finding myself beset by an increasing tendency toward anxiety. Worries about the well-being of our children, about my increasing responsibilities at work, and about the health of our planet kept me from sleeping at night. They began to sap my simple pleasure in being alive. As such anxiety began to shade into a habit of dread, it seemed that Zen practice might be a way to work on myself. Or to step outside of myself.

I feel fortunate to have encountered all these spiritual communities and resources, and to have had the clarity of my wife's own faith as a stabilizing element in our family. Even as I now focus on a Buddhist practice, my past experiences in the Baptist and Quaker communities remain vital for me. These diverse influences combine to create the *aji* of theological incongruity. They offer openings into the majesty of Bible, wilderness, and silence swirling beyond all enclosures. Such a scatter of religious affiliations was not what I had intended, and I feel a little silly telling you about them. But if they haven't quite represented a plan, they do at least feel like a coalescing, if surprising, pattern of connections. Whereas before I identified myself jokingly as a Quatholic, the best I can do at this stage is to describe myself as a Zen Baptist.

There's no doubt that, for professional Go players who can both remember hundreds of games in their entirety and think many moves ahead, *aji* is a carefully calibrated effect. Stones are planted and abandoned deep in an opponent's territory so that they can implicitly pose a threat throughout the game. Even if they never actually spring to life, they will have had their effect. For me, though, with so much more tenuous a grasp on the strategies of Go, the *aji* of my own or the other player's stones often comes as a revelation. It's like a shoot that pushes up through the gummy old leaves of last fall when the intervening snow has finally melted, or like a vole that darts unexpectedly past our toes when we are strolling through an unmown hay field.

This last image relates to an occasion when I heard Gary Snyder describe his own approach to reading as a "hover-and-snatch" process. Rather than pursuing a well-marked authorial track from one side of the field to the other, he will glide above a book like a hawk, alert for a rustling in the grasses that tells him where to plummet for nourishment. Such an independent and improvisatory approach to reading and writing, family life and teaching, is one which I can identify with. As I think about the image and contemplate my jumbled shelves, I come to understand that the hawk is shaped by the biology of the field as surely as the other way around. In my own life, too, the turnings that might have felt like divergence from my origins—both as a teacher of modernist novels and as the child of a Southern Baptist family—could also be seen as instances of being *shaped,* choice after choice, by affinities sprouting from those roots.

In A. R. Ammons's great poem "Corsons Inlet," he takes a walk along the Jersey Shore to give himself to and enter into what he calls "a congregation / rich with entropy." His sacramental language, and his celebration of a world of dunes, grass, and wind through which beautiful shorebirds dart, affirm the surprises of an individual life and a living world. Amid unpredictability, Ammons writes, there is still a "disorderly order." The essays composing the present little book could be characterized as three *landscapes* that I continue to take walks in and to be renewed by. This first one is framed by the tangled, third-growth woods of Vermont and the discourse of wilderness and culture that is germinating in it. My second essay prowls around the topography defined by the books that have been formative for me—a circumambulation I might never have undertaken without the invitation to contribute to this series. And the third tells about our family's decision to buy land in the town next to Bristol and build a sugarhouse on it—both as a new adventure and as a way of consolidating our gathering sense that we belong together here.

Three more days have passed, and I've now hiked out yet again into the portion of the Green Mountain National Forest south of Bread Loaf that has been proposed as a new wilderness area. A coalition of Vermont environmental groups is suggesting that this be called the Romance Mountain Wilderness. Such an act of preservation would honor a man who tried to protect these mountains as forever wild almost a century ago. To tell the story of Joseph Battell is to evoke the surprising reversals of Vermont's environmental history. Wilderness has reemerged here from the clear-cutting and abandonments of the past two centuries, in a succession as vivid as the jewelweed crowding into an unused logging road. Such a transformation in our local landscape enriches the national conversation about nature and culture.

Thick forests define Vermont today. When our landscape is regarded from the window of a small airplane crossing overhead, the farmland of Addison County, south and west of Middlebury, and the development ringing Burlington both seem insignificant against the landscape's central, dark green billow. But ours is a recovering woodland, not a truly ancient legacy like the still-uncut forests of Oregon. When the first big wave of settlers flooded into this state after the American Revolution, they deforested the mountains at an astounding rate. They often cut trees less to clear their fields than to raise cash and supplement the produce of their farms. They burned the logs to make charcoal for the bloomery furnaces of Vermont's active iron industry or to produce potash. By the decade before the Civil War, Vermont had been 80 percent deforested. When Zadock Thompson wrote his natural history of the state in 1853, he found an ecological wasteland, its ravaged slopes no longer providing habitat for most of the larger indigenous animals. Thompson declared not only catamounts and bears, but even beaver and white-tailed deer to be effectively extinct here.

This was the Vermont into which Joseph Battell was born in 1839. Settling on a farm near Bread Loaf in the late 1860s and remaining there until his death in 1915, Battell observed a dramatic process of succession within this scene of devastation. One notable fact for him was the remarkable speed of natural reforestation. After the first clearances, Addison County had seen a burst of sheep farming, known as the Merino Madness. But when that phase had passed, the sheep pastures quickly reverted to woods. White pines, which germinate well in grass as long as they have plenty of sun, dominated this second-growth forest. By the end of the nineteenth century, though, Battell saw a new wave of logging around his Ripton home. In 1891, he called upon the state legislature to save Vermont's forests from "timber butchers, lumber merchants, and firebugs." In fact, though much of Vermont would still be cut over in the decades after this call, Battell did a great deal to buffer those effects. As the largest private landowner in Vermont, and as a passionate proponent of the "forever wild" ethic, he was able to plant the seeds for future wildness in his state.

A key figure in celebrating Battell's legacy has been Jim Northup, who heads Green Mountain Forest Watch. Northup, a former planner for the National Forest, has also served as an adjunct faculty member at Middlebury College and the University of Vermont. In a 1998 seminar for senior Environmental Studies majors at Middlebury, the students and he began to delve both into Battell's history and, more specifically, into the terms of his will. One outgrowth of that research was an essay Northup published in the Summer 1999 issue of *Wild Earth,* entitled "Joseph Battell: Once and Future Wildlands Philanthropist." The story that emerges in this carefully documented account is as intricate, surprising, and, finally, promising as that of Vermont's forest history itself. It shows how the deepest wishes of one visionary preservationist, though thwarted in much of the century since his death, may finally be on the verge of fulfillment today.

Joseph Battell attempted, in his carefully constructed will, to assure that much of the land surrounding Bread Loaf Mountain would be preserved as "a specimen of the original Vermont forest." But after his death in 1915, the first inheritor, Middlebury College, as well as the U.S. Forest Service, which subsequently purchased the bulk of that forestland from the college, struggled to make sense of the bequest. By the lights of their own time, and within the context of their own economic pressures, they didn't see how they could responsibly "operate" the forest without at least some commercial cutting. But I'm not inclined to read either bad faith or a defeat of Battell's "forever wild" dream into the eighty-five years that have passed between his death and the present wilderness proposal. Rather, I see a dramatic process of succession, in which certain crucial pieces of literature and legislation have changed our cultural landscape as well as our natural environment.

I find grounds for hope in the progression

through which Joseph Battell's vision has come to seem clear, compelling, and practical in ways it did not for his contemporaries. Thirty-four years after Battell's startling bequest, Aldo Leopold's *Sand County Almanac* was published. Its chapters "Thinking Like a Mountain" and "The Land Ethic," especially, laid the foundation for the 1964 Wilderness Act. In 1975— eleven years after that landmark legislation and sixty years after Battell's death—the Eastern Wild Areas Act was passed with the leadership of Vermont's Senator George Aiken. Natural areas east of the Mississippi that were neither "vast," "untrammeled," nor "pristine," but that nonetheless had important biological, recreational, or aesthetic qualities, were eligible for full protection as wilderness. Battell's writings and legacy were tendrils in a long process of recovery that has matured into the forest of our present-day wilderness system. The wilderness movement may be said to have germinated in the East, through the contributions of such figures as Thoreau, George Perkins Marsh, and their disciple Battell. Over the last quarter century, it has circled back to this region after its dramatic growth in the mountainous West and Alaska. At the same time, I believe that our vision of wilderness is more than just *confirmed* by its recent application in the East. This may also be an opportunity for it to move one step closer to the true richness and mystery of old growth. Such a further development seems to me, in Leopold's memorable phrase, "an evolutionary possibility and an ecological necessity."

The wilderness ethic has affirmed values in

nature that transcend narrow definitions of human utility. I believe that it and jazz may be America's most important contributions to world culture. Jazz has continued to evolve as new generations of musicians celebrate and build upon the innovations of their ancestors. At one point New Orleans, at another Chicago or Kansas City or New York, have been the venues for breakthroughs in the jazz imagination. So, too, our thinking about wilderness will naturally grow and change. California, Wyoming, New Mexico, and Alaska have been among the places the wilderness ethic has matured, and Vermont may now have a contribution of its own. This may be a place where the future vitality of wilderness is registered and where, given the small scale of official wilderness areas here, it can be understood within a larger ecology of environmental thought.

Six wilderness areas have already been established in Vermont since passage of the 1975 Eastern Wild Areas Act, one of them in my own family's town of Bristol. And shortly after the research carried out by Jim Northup's Environmental Studies seminar, the Middlebury Trustees voted to manage most of the college's remaining acreage from the Battell bequest as "forever wild." I feel hopeful that legislation will soon be passed directing the Forest Service to take a similar step in the much larger portion it owns. Joseph Battell himself took a long view of the cultural change represented by our wilderness movement. In a passage quoted in the *Wild Earth* article, he wrote, "It is very difficult and in some if not many cases impossible for those educated in a system of either politics, science, or religion to relinquish tenets that they have always been instructed in and supposed to be correct. . . . It is therefore a slow process for the world to leave the paths, however erroneous, in which it has long traveled. . . ."

The Romance Mountain Wilderness would be our seventh federally designated wilderness area in Vermont and would form, with Bread Loaf, a contiguous block of approximately fifty thousand acres of preserved forest. This would mean that over 1 percent of the land in Vermont had federal protection as wilderness. My Middlebury colleague Chris McGrory Klyza tells me that the portion thus conserved in some way at federal and state levels would exceed 12 percent. While it has been exciting for those of us here to see these figures increase over the past two decades, they are far from impressive when compared with the percentage of public lands or the acreage of wilderness in some western states. Similarly, the most ardent Vermont environmentalist would admit that the mature groves of spruce and fir above Monastery Peak are far from approximating true old growth. We thus try to assert at every opportunity that the recovery of wildness and the birth of a more inclusive wilderness ethic here in Vermont does not diminish the need to protect ancient forests in Oregon or the Amazon region.

This is a crucial time for dialogue about the meaning of wilderness to the American environmental movement. A group of environmental historians, including William Cronin, has been investigating the political and cultural circumstances out of which the wilderness ideal grew. They sometimes point to instances in which it has been both an expression of economic privilege and an instrument for the disenfranchisement of indigenous groups. Native American writers like Leslie Marmon Silko increasingly challenge the assumption that wilderness is a transcendent value, existing in opposition to the realm of culture. They emphasize the traditional stories—mythic, familial, and personal—that have long been woven into landscapes newcomers might assume to be pristine and primal. Silko's essay "Landscape, History, and the Pueblo Imagination," in particular, has been instructive for me, with its meditation on the ways in which "the ancient people perceived the world and themselves within that world as part of an ancient continuous story composed of innumerable bundles of other stories."

Such critiques have sometimes felt aggravating to wilderness advocates. However, I think that they should be seen instead as opportunities for a more mature, ironic, and inclusive perspective. Environmental stresses of various kinds can trigger powerful surges of successional energy. The sometimes stressful controversies about wilderness may similarly enrich our current dialogue. They pose a fundamental question: What is the larger ecology of environmental thought, within which seeming oppositions might be reconciled? In "Thinking Like a Mountain," Aldo Leopold showed the dangers of a mind-set for which elimination of wolves was the way to preserve the health of deer herds. Just so, we environmentalists need to go beyond the false dichotomies of history versus wilderness, jobs versus the environment. An ecosystem in many ways resembles a vigorous conversation. The dialogue of nature and culture in our time will be advanced both by the revelations that come from solitude in the wilderness and by the insights that come from studying the history of conservation. The wilderness movement itself will be strengthened both by the millions of acres of old growth remaining uncut in the Tongass and by the example of abused woodlands in Vermont straggling back toward wildness and diversity.

Since the days of John Muir and Gifford Pinchot, the opposition between "preservation" and "conservation" has organized much of our thinking. But the size, topography, and settlement history of Vermont may make it easier to think on a whole-landscape scale—to see the preservation of our new wilderness areas as complemented by a variety of environmental efforts in the surrounding regions. I went to a conference not long ago where a wilderness advocate from the Northwest attacked the concept of sustainable forestry. He lampooned such approaches as trying to substitute carob for more caloric, but incomparably more delicious, chocolate. Insofar as I understood his argument, it was that logging of all kinds is hostile to the health of a forest. Thus, the language of sustainability is a delusion, an attempt to reap the benefit of logging without acknowledging its fundamental conflict with conservation—like trying to enjoy the taste of chocolate without consuming all those calories. This presentation angered me because of its obliviousness to conditions in Vermont and much of our region today. While I strongly advocate the expansion of our system of wilderness, I also applaud the development of programs to encourage more sustainable approaches to logging elsewhere in our state. After the conference, I had a chance to reflect more about the Northwest wilderness advocate's presentation and to connect it with the hideous vastness of clear-cuts near his home. I also had to agree with him in much preferring chocolate to carob myself. But I still resist any dichotomy that would blot out the reality, and the promise, of places like Vermont today. Sustainable forestry here feels less like a substitute for wilderness than like a part, with it, of a balanced, nourishing, and varied landscape.

Just as our parks and wildernesses are so much smaller than in the West, so too the pattern of forestry is quite different. Almost 80 percent of the forestlands in Vermont (about 4 million acres) are in private ownership. Over the past quarter century—during which our six wilderness areas were being established—the Vermont Land Trust has bought conservation easements on 324,440 acres of land. This amounts to 6.4 percent of the state's privately owned open land. The past three years have also seen the founding of a new organization called Vermont Family Forests. It promotes green certification for forestlands, along with cooperatives, portable saw-mills, solar kilns, and local, value-added manufac-turing, as a way to give landowners an economic alternative to clear-cutting and subdivision. Such "conservation" initiatives in the working landscape are by no means opposed to the "preservation" of wilderness. Rather, they buffer and connect the wild cores of our state, just as their own biotic and scenic health depends upon those mountainous wilder-nesses at Vermont's heart. Wendell Berry evokes the wholeness of such a vision in his essay "Conserving Forest Communities" when he writes, "Wilderness gives us the indispensable pattern and measure of sustainability."

Forest ecologists speak of the "structure" of a healthy forest. This might be a model through which to visualize the complementarity between our wild-lands and those areas where sustainable forestry and farming are practiced in Vermont. A multiage forest is ecologically richer than a single-age monoculture because different birds, insects, and other creatures find their niches in each distinct understory, thus greatly increasing the forest's biodiversity. Such verti-cal structure also has its horizontal equivalent. As the thick woods thin out to a brushy edge, then give over to a grassy clearing, a greater variety of browse and cover again results. This transitional richness sus-tains mammals needing large quantities of herba-ceous food and offers habitat for ground-nesting animals and birds. It does not mean, despite what some foresters and hunters assert, that the more "edge" the better—as if game species like white-tailed deer and grouse were the only forms of wildlife that counted. Uncut wilderness *between* such edges—wide enough expanses of unbroken canopy, for instance, to support neotropical birds that depend upon them in their migration and nesting—is also essential to a viable forest structure.

The challenge is to put all these elements together in an environmental vision with true ecological breadth. In Vermont, this will mean ambitiously expanding the acreage in totally protected wilderness. Insofar as there is a consensus to continue any cutting at the edges of the National Forest, it must take a modest, single-tree approach and be primarily oriented to sustaining a wide variety of habitats. But it will be equally important for the adjacent private forests and farms to be managed with an eye to environmental protection and restoration and to be seen as protecting our towns from suburban-style sprawl. To miss such potential for complementarity would be a failure of ecological insight. Within the map of a humanly and naturally viable Vermont, the farms and cities alike must be understood in relation to the corridors and buffers that replenish and protect wilderness. The human community's flow of food, energy, and transportation must be coordinated with the migrations, browsing, and reproduction of wildlife. The most beautiful and motivating vision is an inclusive community of life, not wilderness apart from that.

And now, as I take a breather, with my back against a grandmother spruce on Monastery Peak, I paw around in my daypack for lunch. Out come a sandwich, a hunk of cheese, and a bottle of water. No chocolate today. That will be great on another hike. But, for now, I have everything I need right here.

Starting with the Psalms
A READER'S HISTORY

Many authorities on environmental education stress the importance of exposure to nature at an early age. But I have to confide that for me there was a different gate into the flowering world—that of reading. I also need to tell you, here at the outset, that I have never experienced dissonance between the Bible and my environmental ethic. My parents were devout Southern Baptists who took my brother and me to church twice on Sunday as well as on Wednesday night and read the Bible to us at the dinner table. Scriptures like the Psalms grounded my earliest spiritual experiences, inspired my first love of reading, and enhanced my appreciation of the natural world.

I have been surprised, first in college and graduate school and since then during a career of college teaching, that certain academics who would never dream of engaging in other bigoted speech seem to feel comfortable sneering at groups like the Southern Baptists. This strikes me as a classic example of self-ratifying prejudice. Because fundamentalists are assumed to be close-minded, it feels justifiable to discount them as a group. Looking back at my parents' lives across the span of decades and a continent, though, I have to say they were as open, generous, nonmaterialist, and inquisitive as any two people I've ever known. Because I revered and enjoyed them so much even as a child, and because they attached such importance to the activity, I found reading the Bible with my parents to be deeply satisfying. The richness of King James English excited me, for one thing, while the shadowed three-dimensionality of the Genesis tales felt at once more mysterious and more real than any of the other stories I encountered as a boy.

The part of the Bible that most engaged me was the Psalms of David. The image of the shepherd boy who would be King of Israel, alone with his flocks amid the grass and rocks, thrilled me. The evocation of an austere physical routine that at the same time allowed for daily converse with the Lord prepared a place in my heart for backpacking later in life—when the labor of finding water or building fires, sometimes in the wind or under a driving rain, was accompanied by visions of the sunset and the stars. Like many readers over the centuries, I was especially drawn to Psalm 23, which my mother helped me learn by heart before I entered first grade. A picture hung beside my bed with this Psalm inscribed over a picture of Jesus' loving countenance, and with the gentle blues and greens of a spring landscape unfolding behind him.

> The Lord is my shepherd; I shall not want.
> He maketh me to lie down in green pastures: he leadeth me beside the still waters.
> He restoreth my soul: he leadeth me in the paths of righteousness for his name's sake.
> Yea, though I walk through the valley of

the shadow of death, I will fear no evil: for
thou art with me; thy rod and thy staff they
comfort me.

Thou preparest a table before me in the
presence of mine enemies: thou anointest my
head with oil; my cup runneth over.

Surely goodness and mercy shall follow me
all the days of my life: and I will dwell in the
house of the Lord for ever.

Having grown up in the rural South, and having
come of age during the Depression and World War II,
neither of my parents felt much need to sleep outside
after they had arranged for a perfectly sound roof
over our heads. Camping was not us. In some sense,
then, the Psalms were my most vivid early exposure
to natural beauty while growing up in the pleasantly
paved and manicured landscape of suburban California. This may have contributed to my skepticism
upon reading Lynn White Jr.'s influential 1967 essay,
"The Historical Roots of Our Ecologic Crisis," later in
life. In an argument that has often been echoed, he
suggests that many of the environmental problems
of our era can be traced back to the "dominion" language of the Book of Genesis. This has always struck
me as anachronistic, though, in part because the
Psalms made it so clear that the Hebrew scriptures
were grounded in a pastoral culture. To blame sacred
texts originating in an oral tradition thousands of
years ago for the havoc caused by the internal com-
bustion engine, for the current rate of atmospheric

and oceanic damage, for superfund sites, and for the other heedless destructiveness of post–World War II society seems like quite a stretch. What a transparent attempt to exonerate our own generation for the wastefulness of our practices! For a shepherd in ancient Israel, "dominion" on the best of days wouldn't have meant much more than keeping the sheep together. It is certainly true that we need to reconstruct our religious traditions, and in particular to rethink our inherited vocabulary about the relationship between spirit and nature. But I believe that, in its overlapping of historical, lyrical, and prophetic texts, the Bible represents a resource for greater environmental mindfulness, rather than being fundamentally the problem.

In addition to offering my first glimpse of a reflective life amid natural beauty, Psalm 23 first inspired in me a love of poetry. As a little boy I relished the way each verse contained a balanced pair of statements. The pervasiveness of other forms of repetition, as in the second and third verses ("he leadeth me") also gave the Psalm a stately, grand effect to the ear of a child. Not only did the green pastures and still waters pictured in that devotional poster on the wall leave me with a feeling of calm happiness, but the first half of the fourth verse ("Yea, though I walk through the valley of the shadow of death") thrilled me every time I said it aloud, and thrills me yet. It was sublime—over the top. A glimpse of rugged, and potentially fatal, landscapes far from the benign enclosures of childhood and family. The other thing that struck me from the first about this Psalm was how it *moved*. The first three verses described the Lord's kindness in a measured way. But once the emotional tone shifted toward the danger of verse four, the language shifted, too, to a more urgent, intimate address: "for thou art with me." It may seem unrealistic for a child to have noticed such details. But this Psalm and the Lord's Prayer were the first things I had ever memorized. I felt mighty pleased to have them and often, as it were, looked in on them to see how they were doing.

Another aspect of the Psalm's movement that I registered only years afterward was the way the poet plays with his two-part structure in verse five. In this scene of sponsorship and prosperity, there is an extra, third element in the verse. Like the cup, the line itself "runneth over." The part of that particular line that confused me as a boy, though, was the phrase "in the presence of mine enemies." Surrounded as I was by people who were kind to me, I couldn't imagine why the Psalmist had to introduce a dischord of enemies into his idyll. But I can feel now how necessary the reference was, both aesthetically and emotionally. Like Malvolio and the other unreconciled characters at the end of Shakespeare's comedies, it balances the final affirmation ("Surely goodness and mercy shall follow me all the days of my life") and keeps the Psalm from becoming sentimental. I've always enjoyed my father's definition of sentimentality as loving something more than God does. The landscape of this comforting Psalm is far from feeling totally safe—as an anxious reader is shepherded through the valley of the shadow, then invited into the presence of enemies.

Psalm 23 is a touchstone for my experience of literature. It helps me to understand both the continuity and the principle of selectivity within the works that have spoken most powerfully to me over the years. So much strife is generated within literary studies in the academy between those who want to assert the primacy of "the canon" and those who want to open the curriculum up to a more multicultural perspective. But I believe the combatants exaggerate both the antagonism between these two values and, for that matter, the capacity of any individual to fulfill either of them. While I definitely feel the attractiveness of multiculturalism as an ideal, it often strikes me how hard it is to be even *cultural* in anything but the sociological meaning of the term. This is not to undermine the principle itself, to which in fact I subscribe. But a certain modesty would be appropriate in relating ourselves to multiculturalism. We should not assume, in other words, that it is a readily available option of some sort—as if multiculturalism were an easy equivalent to the dozens of TV channels that we can bring into our homes for a monthly check to the cable company.

Similarly, to identify oneself as a champion of the canon, even if that term is limited to literature in English, seems a form of hubris. If two people could agree on what the canon is, and if each of them had actually read and reflected upon all those works, I believe that it would still be impossible for them to bring an equal degree of knowledge and appreciation to every one of those literary masterpieces. I remember a conversation one of my Middlebury colleagues once had with a student who was complaining about a given year's reading list for our senior comprehensive exams. This English major was particularly displeased by the need to study Dryden. The faculty member said, "But Dryden would be seen by many people as one of the ten most influential poets in English." To which his student replied, "Yeah. Number ten." As we repeated this exchange laughingly in the department, its point seemed to be our student's need to transcend the assumptions of a consumerist society and give himself to the magnificent range of English literature. But for most of us, not just that senior English major, the list of authors we intimately know and love would be much shorter than the list we have encountered on a more detached, intellectual level. Amid all the glories of literature, my own central lineage of the heart runs through the writing of Milton and Wordsworth, then opens out into nature writing and contemporary poetry. The overflowing meanings of this particular tradition bring me to a landscape whose beauty is inseparable from the shadows of separation and fear.

A love of Milton has been one of Middlebury College's greatest gifts to me. My classes on *Paradise Lost* as both an undergraduate and a graduate student were dry and unengaging. I reached the conclusion that he was one "major English author" I just couldn't care for. The verse itself struck me as clotted and over determined, while the classroom lectures and discussions never seemed to get much beyond Restoration politics and Puritan theology. The low point came in my first term at Yale Graduate School when I was asked to do an exhaustive study of the secondary literature for a seminar paper I was preparing. Sitting in a dusty carrel of Sterling Library and reading a *PMLA* article entitled "Milton's Use of I and J in Latin Script," I experienced a sharp pang of vocational doubt. That night I called Rita, then in her senior year at Pomona College, from my Mansfield Street boardinghouse. I told her of my decision to flee from the scholarly hive before it was too late. We ultimately reached the decision that, since she was committed for the duration at Pomona anyway, I might as well finish up this one year of grad school. But if I had to do much more reading like that, I should definitely not go back.

Rita and I did end up taking the next year off from school to travel in Africa after our marriage in the summer. But we returned to New Haven, where I completed my Ph.D. in English and then had the good fortune to find a job at Middlebury. Maybe it came simply from being older than when I studied Milton in graduate school, or perhaps it was a result of studying *Paradise Lost* each fall in a small seminar for sophomore majors where the emphasis was on close reading. Whatever the reason, Milton suddenly became, and remains, one of the central landmarks of my literary experience. His vision of human history commencing and progressing (when it does progress) through a "fortunate fall" conveyed a tragic but hopeful vision at the core of our culture. Disasters and violations will come. They are what we humans do. But each of them also represents an opportunity for moral evolution, to the extent that we can muster the energy for a creative response.

I realized at Middlebury that Milton was like Shakespeare in being a microcosmic poet or, as Hugh Kenner would say, a fractal one. Point by point, the details of his verse resonate with his grand themes. Milton's epic similes especially delighted me, as they did my students, with their compression and their remarkable mélange of narratives, emotions, and cultures. One of my grounds for skepticism about the assumed opposition between multiculturalism and the canon is the fact that Milton, at the core of English literature, can synthesize such an extraordinary range of cultural references. And in this, as in other ways, he is one of Shakespeare's aptest disciples. An example of Milton's use of epic similes comes in Book I of *Paradise Lost,* when he evokes the dangerous grandeur of Satan, still stretched out in the fire of hell where God has cast him after the Battle in Heaven.

> Thus Satan, talking to his nearest mate,
> With head uplift above the wave, and eyes
> That sparkling blazed; his other parts besides,
> Prone on the flood, extended long and large,
> Lay floating many a rood, in bulk as huge
> As whom the fables name of monstrous size,

Titanian, or Earth-born, that warred on Jove,
Briareos or Typhon, whom the den
By ancient Tarsus held, or that sea-beast
Leviathan, which God of all his works
Created hugest that swim the ocean-stream.
Him, haply, slumbering on the Norway foam
The pilot of some small night-foundered skiff
Deeming some island, oft, as seamen tell,
With fixèd anchor in his scaly rind,
Moors by his side under the lee, while night
Invests the sea, and wished morn delays.

The two words typifying Milton's approach in this epic of a sentence are "as" and "or." "As" is the language of analogy that lends such resonance to the entire poem. The classical authors' accounts of Titans warring against Jove prefigured, for a Christian writer like Milton, the rebellion against God by Satan and his followers. The reference to Tarsus—the site in Asia Minor where Jove imprisoned the Giant Typhon, one of the Titans' monstrous offspring, anticipates the defeat and humiliation of Satan by God. But these comparisons also emphasize the size and power of Satan, against the glamorous backdrop of ancient literature, and contribute much to the sublime, dark beauty of Milton's own verse. We are fascinated by Satan's magnitude. Even when the allusions cluster so thickly that they complicate and interrupt the main description, they enhance its overall effect. Edmund Burke, inspired in part by the example of *Paradise Lost,* pointed out a century later that the supreme experiences of art or nature that we call "sublime" often result from extremes of size, obscurity, and danger. This positive association with terms that might have seemed negative leads to that second word, "or."

Milton multiplies his analogies in part because of the ecstatic fertility of his imagination, but also because he wants to make sure that his reader doesn't miss the doctrinal point amid all the glories of his language. In effect, he breaks into the buzzing room of his poetry with an urgent message, and in this sort of interjection he anticipates Gary Snyder and Mary Oliver among our contemporaries. He vaults from ancient Greece and Asia Minor to the seas off Norway in order to escape from the gravitational pull of the previous imagery, and to insist that any reader fascinated by the fabulous immensity of Satan should be all the more wary of trusting in his power. That would be incomparably more dangerous than mooring one's skiff to the "scaly rind" of a slumbering whale in northern seas.

Milton's vision of redemption, too, is rendered more vivid by the dark sublimity of Satan. In Book XII, after the Archangel Michael has shown him the pageant of suffering and resurrection that human history will bring, Adam can exclaim:

O Goodness infinite, Goodness immense!
That all this good of evil shall produce,
And evil turn to good; more wonderful
Than that which by creation first brought forth
Light out of darkness! Full of doubt I stand,
Whether I should repent me now of sin

By me done and occasioned, or rejoice
Much more, that much more good thereof
    shall spring;
To God more glory, more good-will to men
From God, and over wrath grace shall abound.

This passage always makes me think of the Dutch graphic artist M. C. Escher. Within one of Escher's typically packed designs, white birds dive, dark fish rise, outlining and defining each other, inseparable. Milton's esthetic and his theology similarly arise from the unity of contrasts. No Satan, no Christ; no danger, no transfiguration. John Muir, in the realm of American nature writing, also felt this aspect of Milton's appeal. *Paradise Lost* and Emerson's *Essays* were the two books Muir carried in his pack when setting out to walk from Wisconsin to the Gulf of Mexico. I believe that he found in Milton, as I too have discovered, a bridge between his early religious training and the wider world of literature. But the dangerous sublimity of Satan may also have prepared Muir for the grand precariousness of mountain travel. In *The Mountains of California,* Muir describes avalanches and windstorms of titanic force, as well as moments when he had climbed into such peril that he thought he was lost. Such danger was never the *main* reality for him. The Sierra Nevada was above all "the Range of Light," "divinely beautiful." But without the shadow of danger and the challenges of physical exertion, the light could not have struck him as (to use Muir's favorite adjective) so utterly "glorious."

Muir's early exposure to the Bible did not come in a home as benign as the one I was so fortunate to grow up in. His Scots Calvinist father beat John daily, not only for the sins he had committed but also for those of which he *might* have been guilty. This abuse was coupled with study of the Scriptures. So that by the time he moved on from his father's Wisconsin homestead, Muir had learned all of the New Testament and much of the Old Testament "by heart and sore flesh." John Muir's childhood seems to have been, in this regard, a shadow from which he stepped into the luminous beauty of Yosemite and "the Range of Light." In his emotional life, as in his prowess as a climber and his acuteness as an observer of nature, Muir lived at extremes. But even for those whose lives aren't so marked by stark highs and lows, the difficulty, the discomfort, certainly, and occasionally even the danger of personal expeditions into wild country may frame and intensify our experience of natural beauty. Such tribulations open us up, scouring away our mechanical habits of perception and alerting us to the sublime tides that surge through every day. The presence of enemies near the table of goodness and mercy is one detail of Psalm 23 expressing this deep, yet perpetually surprising, affinity. In nature and literature alike, the sublime shadows our experience, rounding it into the three-dimensionality of a world with room for our human hearts.

In our own day, Milton's drama of darkness and light flows into both the poetry of the earth in English and the achievements of nature writing. The many affinities of these two modern genres, but especially their shared alertness to the light that blazes out of darkness, sometimes make me see them as a single tradition. I don't say this in a spirit of detached literary judgment. It is, rather, my grateful testimony to a lineage of books that have guided and enriched my life. These are works of prophetic beauty, grounded in the insight that literature itself is a landscape; conversely, as we walk across the outward landscape, bearing with us an open mind and heart, we may learn to read more deeply.

Wordsworth was the inheritor of Milton's moral vision and his psychological acuteness. Onto them he grafted an autobiographical narrative, framed by the distinctive topography and seasons of a beloved landscape, that has become a central structure for nature writing and poetry in our own century. The Romantic movement, of which Wordsworth was one of the founders in England, has often been seen as subverting the hierarchical values of the preceding, neoclassical era. Reacting against that centralized realm of values, with its sense of authority and achievement emanating from the artistic establishments of Rome, Paris, and London, the Romantics proposed a democratic and, one might say, ecological alternative. Folktales, ballads, dreams, and the emotional lives of children were seen as having meaning potentially even greater than the rationalistic perspectives of an educated and affluent elite. Such a romantic-neoclassical contrast goes far to explain Wordsworth's and Coleridge's strategies in *The Lyrical Ballads,* for instance. But I have been drawn to a more specific connection between Wordsworth and Milton, on the one hand, and between Wordsworth and the poets and nature writers succeeding him on the other. This is the celebration, within the entire lineage, of light as the writer's central subject, and of darkness, in the spiritual and social sense as well as the physical, as its necessary context.

A central example of this pattern in Wordsworth appears in Book VI of *The Prelude*—which is also the work that most directly anticipates American nature writing. As the speaker is hiking in the Alps, eager to reach the highest pass and know that he is standing on the roof of Europe, he suddenly realizes that he has already, unknowingly, crossed the main ridge. Any traveler in the mountains learns how hard it is to assess the relative height of surrounding summits, given the potential deceptions of distance, perspective, angle, and light. The speaker here, who had been looking forward to a peak experience while astride the pass, instead must shamble down the trail with his hopes dashed. But this moment of "melancholy slackening" turns out, astonishingly, to be when the landscape erupts in meaning.

> Downwards we hurried fast,
> And, with the half-shaped road which we had
>   missed,
> Entered a narrow chasm. The brook and road
> Were fellow-travellers in this gloomy strait,
> And with them did we journey several hours
> At a slow pace. The immeasurable height

Of woods decaying, never to be decayed,
The stationary blasts of waterfalls,
And in the narrow rent at every turn
Winds thwarting winds, bewildered and
　　forlorn,
The torrents shooting from the clear blue sky,
The rocks that muttered close upon our ears,
Black drizzling crags that spake by the way-side
As if a voice were in them, the sick sight
And giddy prospect of the raving stream,
The unfettered clouds and region of the
　　Heavens,
Tumult and peace, the darkness and the light—
Were all like workings of one mind, the
　　features
Of the same face, blossoms upon one tree;
Characters of the great Apocalypse,
The types and symbols of Eternity,
Of first, and last, and midst, and without end.

Wordsworth's ecstatic revelations amid the heights anticipate Muir's "Range of Light." But his ironic awareness of the way in which false expectations may be the context and, in effect, the preparation for visionary moments is more fully registered in a contemporary work like Annie Dillard's *Pilgrim at Tinker Creek*. Rita gave me this book for Christmas in 1977, and it immediately rearranged my sense of literature, lending a new direction to my reading, teaching, and writing. My parents had presented me with a copy of *Walden* on my fifteenth birthday— fifteen years before Rita's gift. All those years I had treasured Thoreau's prose, transcribing favorite selections of "Spring" and "Higher Laws" into my journal and reading them aloud to friends. But no other masterpiece of creative nonfiction had ever come into my ken: I had assumed *Walden* was unique—the only book on that particular shelf. *Pilgrim at Tinker Creek* finally felt like another one to lean beside it, though, both in the nature of its voice and themes and in the excellence of its prose.

In the second chapter of her book, which is entitled "Seeing," Dillard writes of a girl blind from birth who is given sight by a new form of surgery. This celebrated passage introduces a leitmotif for the whole book—of the quest to see the world as vividly as a person who is newly sighted.

> When her doctor took her bandages off and led her into the garden, the girl who was no longer blind saw "the tree with the lights in it." It was for this tree I searched through the peach orchards of summer, in the forests of fall and down winter and spring for years. Then one day I was walking along Tinker Creek thinking of nothing at all and I saw the tree with the lights in it. I saw the backyard cedar where the mourning doves roost charged and transfigured, each cell buzzing with flame. I stood on the grass with the lights in it, grass that was wholly fire, utterly focused and utterly dreamed. It was less like seeing than like being for the first time seen, knocked breathless by a powerful glance. The flood of fire abated, but I'm still

spending the power. Gradually the lights went out in the cedar, the colors died, the cells unflamed and disappeared. I was still ringing. I had been my whole life a bell, and never knew it until at that moment I was lifted and struck. I have since only very rarely seen the tree with the lights in it. The vision comes and goes, mostly goes, but I live for it, for the moment when the mountains open and a new light roars in spate through the crack, and the mountains slam.

From the moment I first read this passage and entered into the tangled, funny, alarming skein of Dillard's reflections and narratives, I too was hungry for such intensity. Inspired by Dillard, I renewed my practices of journal-keeping, drawing, and botanizing. They were ways to pursue the goal of seeing the world vividly, of glimpsing life more abundant. I also eagerly explored contemporary American nature writing and began to integrate more and more of it into my teaching. I discovered how central to this body of literature was the hunger for visionary experience that Scott Slovic has defined as "seeking awareness." From Edward Abbey to Barry Lopez and Terry Tempest Williams, the shadows of deprivation and estrangement, historical folly and personal grief, function to make the moments of connection more dazzling, to convey the possibility for transfiguration. This Wordsworthian element also flows into American nature writing through Emerson, who writes in *Nature*, "If the stars should appear one night in a thousand years, how would men believe and adore; and preserve for many generations the remembrance of the city of God which had been shown!" A certain "impoverishment," as Emerson might say, may stimulate the capacity for wonder. One basic difference between Emerson and our latter-day American visionaries, though, is that for many of them the darkness around their moments of revelation also includes a world of ecological catastrophe. This chastened awareness is part of the special value of such writers for readers of today. They acknowledge the perils and the horrors of natural degradation while also celebrating the rewards that can come to one who, in Scott Russell Sanders's memorable phrase, is "hunting for hope."

"The tree with the lights in it" is a phrase that sums up much of what has stirred me in American nature writing. "The narrow road" is another key phrase for me, expressing the enormous value I have found in contemporary poets like Gary Snyder, A. R. Ammons, and Mary Oliver—as well as in the haiku tradition of Bashō with which they have such a deep, if mysterious, connection. That latter phrase comes in fact from the title of Bashō's masterpiece intertwining haiku with travel narrative, *Oku no Hosomichi* ("The Narrow Road to the Interior"). I was first led to Bashō, as to the study of Japanese and to the sabbatical my family and I spent in Japan, through admiration for our American contemporary Gary Snyder. The poetry of Snyder, one of the first Westerners to pursue Zen in a Japanese monastery, offered a stringent counter-point to the Miltonic tradition. His voice both baffled and impressed me. I wanted to learn where he came from by exploring the Zen-based literature and culture of Japan.

I quickly encountered Bashō's *The Narrow Road,* a poetic account of traveling as determined and courageous as it was pervaded by melancholy. The narrative, as translated by Noboyuki Yuasa, begins memorably.

> Days and months are travellers of eternity. So are the years that pass by. Those who steer a boat across the sea, or drive a horse over the earth till they succumb to the weight of years, spend every minute of their lives travelling. There are a great number of ancients, too, who died on the road. I myself have been tempted for a long time by the cloud-moving wind— filled with a strong desire to wander.

The world, and time itself, are travelers. To travel with them is to embrace, and perhaps also to hasten, one's own mortality. Surrendering to the passage of time may be attractive in part because of the ways loss and death themselves seem to offer openings into nature. The gentle sadness, or *sabi,* so character-istic of Japanese poetry registers a doubleness that is oddly akin to the dual impact of the sublime in Western thought. An awareness of one's own fading life, like the passing of springtime, is the soil in which a deeper sympathy may germinate. One of the most famous haiku in this volume of Bashō's describes the poet's response to the scene of a famous sequence of battles five centuries earlier.

> Indeed, many a feat of chivalrous valour was repeated here during the short span of the three generations, but both the actors and the deeds have long been dead and passed into oblivion. When a country is defeated, there remain only mountains and rivers, and on a ruined castle in spring only grasses thrive. I sat down on my hat and wept bitterly till I almost forgot time.

> Summer grass—
> all that remains
> of warriors' dreams.

Though the poet weeps at this scene of failed hopes, he also continually searches out such affecting locales in *The Narrow Road*. They seem, in fact, to provide one of the aged poet's main reasons for traveling so far on foot. Perhaps he finds reassurance as well as sorrow in the supplanting of human hopes by grasses bending under the wind. The prose passage leading up to the haiku echoes the famous line of Tu Fu, "Though the capital may fall, the mountains and rivers remain." Having been led to Bashō by a poet of our own day, I have also been given a heightened awareness of how contemporary writers, too, pace the earth in quest of visions. And of how, like him, they sometimes find in the frailty of human achievements the confirmation of a deeper, sustaining faith.

Many poems by Gary Snyder speak to this point, offering readers a broader historical perspective so that we can better orient ourselves amid the imbalances of the present. A poem of his that has been central for me is "For the Children," from *Turtle Island.*

The rising hills, the slopes,
of statistics
lie before us.
the steep climb
of everything, going up,
up, as we all
go down.

In the next century
or the one beyond that,
they say,
are valleys, pastures,
we can meet there in peace
if we make it.

To climb these coming crests
one word to you, to
you and your children:

stay together
learn the flowers
go light

Bashō's haiku about the grass of warrior's dreams recalls ancient battles in a landscape that has, apparently, forgotten them. But "For the Children" stands at the edge of an *approaching* catastrophe—in a world of "everything, going up, / up, as we all / go down." This poem limns the graph of our time, as use of fossil fuels, eradication of wild habitat, damage to atmospheric and oceanic systems, and human population all curve steeply up. In all such exponential graphs, along with the visible x- and y-axes, an invisible line defines the right margin. This is the "asymptote" toward which the curve grows closer and closer without ever touching it. Such an upward thrust represents a fantasy of endless growth, blasting through gravitation and the other limits of our earth. But another invisible line implicitly cuts across the top of the graph and establishes the limited carrying capacity of our earth. Some economists refer to those who assert such limits as "catastrophians," in contrast to their own "cornucopian" faith, which asserts that market demands and technological ingenuity will always generate replacements for dwindling resources. But we are looking toward a world of 11 billion people within my children's generation. Most of the growth is projected for the poorest countries, while the wealthiest pursue a binge of consumerism that skews the distribution of the world's goods ever more grotesquely. A recent *World Watch* report entitled *Beyond Malthus* states that, even at present population levels, it would take eight more earths to make a middle-class American lifestyle conceivable for all of humanity. One wonders where the self-styled cornucopians might expect to find these new planets.

It is plain to the speaker in Snyder's poem, at any rate, that the curve must turn back down. Either we will bend it down by forethought, discipline, and re-structuring of our economic and social systems, or those systems will crash and we will come back down to earth in some faster way. This latter prospect casts "the shadow of death" across Snyder's poem. But the speaker here, as in Psalm 23, can also look beyond the perilous present—to "the next century / or the one beyond that," when the planet and its human inhabitants will one way or another come back into balance. The poem crosses over the high passes of our current peril and descends into the habitable valleys of the future. This is the point where a reader can see the opening graph of heedlessness transformed into the beautiful balance of an ancient Chinese or Japanese ink painting. Snyder substitutes the simplicity of a walk and a poem for the self-destructive indulgence of our day. This is another way in which he resembles Bashō, who took to the road in order to renew his own culture's sensitivity to nature, at a time when the Zen-based arts were largely presided over by esthetes within the enclosed compounds of privilege.

Poetry is primarily an experience rather than a statement of fact. But one element I love in a poem like "For the Children" is the simplicity and direct-ness of its ending: *"stay together / learn the flowers / go light."* As the Wordsworthian tradition has entered a world of ecological disasters, a prophetic voice regularly punctuates its cadences—like the pause to look and think that interrupts and shapes a hike. The ending of "For the Children," like many passages in contemporary American poetry, resonates with "The Land Ethic," from Aldo Leopold's *A Sand County Almanac*. In that essay, Leopold sees culture on the verge of recognizing "rights" beyond the human circle. Such an expansion of our ethical perspective, he says, has become "an evolutionary possibility and an ecological necessity."

Snyder's poem, with its similar awareness of the ecological moment, expresses the eagerness to wake up that has long throbbed in America's nature writing as well as in our poetry of the earth. Thoreau writes in "Where I Lived and What I Lived For" that "We must learn to reawaken and keep ourselves awake, not by mechanical aids, but by an infinite expectation of the dawn." He adds, "Only that day dawns to which we are awake." Mary Oliver, in her poem "Turtle," evokes a pond in which a snapping turtle rises slowly toward the soft beauty of teal chicks. She breaks into her own rising sense of horror, though, to ask and answer a question that reorients her both as a poet and a citizen of nature.

> But, listen,
> what's important?
> Nothing's important
>
> except that the great and cruel mystery of the world,
> of which this is a part,
> not be denied. . . .

Such admonishing, inspiring voices have made all the difference in my life. Confused as I have generally been about matters of theology, as well as about where my path is and which way I am supposed to be walking on it anyway, a brisk reminder to wake up to the present can feel life saving. Here, too, the testimony of contemporary American literature is amplified for me by the Zen tradition that informs Bashō's poetry. One of the chants used during times of *sesshin,* or intensive retreat, at many American Zen centers is the Zazen Wasan, or "Master Hakuin's Chant in Praise of Zazen." One stanza of it goes:

How near the truth
Yet how far we seek,
Like one in water crying "I thirst!"
Like a child of rich birth
Wand'ring poor on this earth,
We endlessly circle the six worlds.

Just as Snyder's poetry and Bashō's have felt mutually illuminating, so too I have found that Japan's haiku tradition has brought me back to our Vermont poet Robert Frost with renewed appreciation. It is characteristic of haiku to imply a specific seasonal reference. One of my favorite haiku by Bashō goes *"Kare eda ni / karasu no tomarikeri / aki no fure"* (On a withered branch / alights a crow, / the end of autumn). Within each season there are seasons. Peter Milward in fact translates the haiku's last line "the fall of autumn" in order to emphasize this point. The spring of autumn, one might say, comes when colors bloom in the hardwoods; its summer, in the golden needles of the tamarack. But when most deciduous trees have become bare and the only tonality in the sky is the crow that alights to make the bough bounce once under its weight (Bashō's onomatopoetic *tomarikeri*), one experiences the season's completion and culmination. Haiku rarely depict peacocks or other conventionally gorgeous natural objects. Rather, they mark a particular moment in the turning year and bring into sharp resolution a single object in the world. As they hone in on the awkward, incongruous, or homely instances that are the haiku poets' stock-in-trade, these brief strings of syllables suggest that anything in the world we can truly see will contain everything we need. Like Thoreau's world in which dawn and spring are both perpetually available for one who is awake, haiku offer a meaningful, and entirely adequate, world waiting for our notice. Bashō was a poet, not a priest, and was careful to specify that, though trained in a monastery, he had never attained enlightenment. But the stanza quoted above from Zen Master Hakuin echoes his vision of a world thronging with haiku that need only to be perceived.

Dillard specifies that she finally sees the tree with the lights in it when she is wandering beside Tinker Creek "thinking of nothing at all." One of the most valuable contrasts between Bashō and my beloved Milton and Wordsworth is his avoidance of arguments, logical propositions, and elaborations of all kinds. Another haiku by him goes *"Meigetsu ya— / ike wo megurite, / mo yoh sugara—"* (Full moon of autumn— / all night long / I walk around the pond). *Meigetsu,* the "famous moon," appears at the end of each September. Japanese devotees of the haiku tradition love to recite poems that are closely associated with such highly specific seasons through which they are passing. Sometimes they write them out on long thin placards of wood and hang them from trees to participate in a tradition of responsiveness to nature.

Bashō and his lineage have helped me recognize how many of Robert Frost's poems encounter our own Vermont landscape with an equivalent vividness and specificity. Snowshoeing around Bristol and Starksboro in those January and February weeks when the evergreens are packed with snow, I love to pause by a hemlock, push on a branch with my ski pole until it releases the small drift that freighted it, and say Frost's little poem "Dust of Snow."

> The way a crow
> Shook down on me
> The dust of snow
> From a hemlock tree
>
> Has given my heart
> A change of mood
> And saved some part
> Of a day I had rued.

This poem entered into my heart several years ago, on a day when the tracker Sue Morse was taking a group of my students and me around her land at Wolf Run. She recited it as we all paused beside a snowy hemlock, in what was for everyone a striking moment. When I do the same with other groups of students now, I feel that I am entering into a lineage of celebration—of the place, the poem, and all the people who have loved both of them before me.

Another poem of Frost's that serves as an important marker of the Vermont year is "Nothing Gold Can Stay." Growing up in the San Francisco Bay Area, I did not encounter such strongly marked seasons as we know in Vermont. But an arresting seasonality has become central to my sense of place here. When Rita and I were in graduate school in New Haven, our last year before moving to Vermont, we lived in a third-floor apartment on an old-fashioned street called Sheldon Terrace. As spring arrived and we were already beginning to box up our books and otherwise anticipate graduation and a move, we looked out our front windows, right into the top of one of the mature maples that lined the sidewalk. It seemed to be full of crisp yellow flowers—beautiful, intricate, and unfamiliar. We gazed at them, even opening the windows to lean out and get closer, before figuring out that we were really witnessing the moment when the buds opened and the new leaves emerged. The tiny new leaves, not yet greened up in the sun, pushed out of the sheath with all their tips and angles clustered together in a lacy bloom for the first day or so. Frost's poem helped us to place this phenomenon, and to remember it again, here in Vermont, each spring.

> Nature's first green is gold,
> Her hardest hue to hold.
> Her early leaf's a flower,

But only so an hour.
Then leaf subsides to leaf,
So Eden sank to grief.
So dawn goes down to day.
Nothing gold can stay.

Even in such a short poem, a Western poet like Frost will usually reflect about his observations in ways that Japanese poets would avoid—preferring to leave such reflections up to the reader. In this sense, perhaps only the third line of Frost's poem is really a haiku. But I love the rest of it too, especially the line "Then leaf subsides to leaf." Each season is both an arrival and a departure, and what we see is always a process. There is a sadness in the ceaseless turning of our living world, as well as in the literature of nature, that reverberates with Virgil's lines in the *Aeneid* about "the tears of things, mortal affairs that touch the mind." For Virgil, these tears arise both from the inevitable sunderings of human history and from the evanescence of all life. The beautiful forms of nature are the traces of life's passing. But the arising and subsiding of life is also its fulfillment. Without it there would be no leaf, no gold, no mystery in the spring treetops. From a poem like "Nothing Gold Can Stay" to those like "In Hardwood Groves" and "The Leaf Treader," Frost focuses on each phase of the foliage's annual cycle of unfolding, greening, reddening, and fall. As he says in "In Hardwood Groves," "the same leaves over and over again." The landscape's arc—up, across, and down—from spring to fall gives us human inhabitants a yearly opportunity to identify our own mortality with the integrity and beauty of the landscape, to ground ourselves and let ourselves go.

I once had an experience in the late September woods near Bread Loaf that related both to Bashō and to Frost. The Dalai Lama was visiting Middlebury College for several days as a participant in a Buddhist-Christian dialogue. I was asked, as a wildflower fancier, to take him and his entourage on a walk through the woods to see some fall blooms. I was of course excited to do so. The wrinkle was that someone in the college's public affairs office had told the press about the event, and when we arrived at the trailhead, a cluster of photographers was waiting. They backed ahead of us as we strolled, shutters crackling like brushfire. Then, as we paused to inspect a stand of steeplebush beside our path, a particularly brash photographer stooped over to pick up a crimson maple leaf, thrust it into the Dalai Lama's hands, saying, "Here, your Holiness," then stood back expectantly with his camera. The Dalai Lama inspected the leaf carefully, then held it forward for the photographer to see, while saying the single word, "Transience." It was a teaching of the Dharma, and a quiet celebration of the wholeness of nature. It was an echo of Bashō, there on a path where Robert Frost had also walked with an eye out for the leaves.

The other influence on my growing love for Frost's poetry has been the decision Rita and I reached about a decade ago to make this region of the Green Mountains our home for the rest of our lives. We had always appreciated the beauty of this landscape and loved our teaching here, mine at Middlebury College and hers at the Lincoln Community School. But, as Californians, without thinking much about it, we had always seen this location as temporary. Our extended families were still in the West, and the world was full of places we might want to go, jobs we might want to hold. Having enjoyed ourselves in this mode for over fifteen years, though, we gradually realized that Vermont was where we were in fact *living*. Our children had grown up entirely here, and these seasons had shaped our adult lives since the completion of our formal education. Recognizing and celebrating this fact, and deciding that, quite independent of our specific teaching jobs, we would never leave our home here, has felt so liberating. Like a commitment to marriage, our decision removed a range of potential distractions, allowing us to deepen a chosen and committed relationship with place.

One immediate upshot of our decision was, for me, a desire to study the natural history and human history of Vermont more systematically. While hiking around the nearby mountains and reading the chronicles of early settlers here, I kept a journal in which the poetry of Frost came to play an unexpected and notable role. Not only was he a fine naturalist and an observer of the shifting seasons, he was also alert to the twists and reversals of settlement here. He saw northern New England as a postagricultural region, one where many of the hill farmers had already left and where the forests were crowding back in. Such a landscape, for Frost, offered an opportunity to meditate about the relationship between wilderness and culture, and about loss as the vehicle for a deeper sense of history and community. The hardwood groves where hill farms were once maintained stirred him as the summer grass of warriors' dreams did Bashō.

Of all Frost's poems, the one that most informed my sense of our family's home was "Directive," from the 1946 volume *Steeple Bush*. Its opening, especially, captured this paradoxical landscape of loss and recovery.

> Back out of all this now too much for us,
> Back in a time made simple by the loss
> Of detail, burned, dissolved, and broken off
> Like graveyard marble sculpture in the weather,
> There is a house that is no more a house
> Upon a farm that is no more a farm
> And in a town that is no more a town.

Vermont is a state where wilderness is recovering—as registered by both the burgeoning of wildlife and the designation of portions of our Green Mountain National Forest as federal wilderness areas. Such lands, preserved from further development, motorized transport, and permanent human habitation, may feel like refuges from history. Like islands of serenity and solitude where we can escape from the modern world's "all this now too much for us." But we sometimes take a foreshortened view and separate wilderness from history in a way that runs the risk of sentimentality. Ours can be a vision "made simple by the loss / Of detail." Paying attention to the relics of former inhabitants in these mountains, to the stone walls, cellar holes, and abandoned graveyards, we may achieve a more integrated awareness of what it means to dwell here. Frost has helped me to begin paying such attention to our family's home ground.

From the Psalms to the poets and nature writers of our own day, literature has offered me a connection both with a grounded lineage of human feelings and with the landscape that stimulated and still fosters such response. This continuity is a form of grace, and one for which I want to return thanks all the days of my life.

Sugaring Off

Here it is, the second week of March 2000, and the sap is running. The last six months have been absorbed by building a sugarhouse and preparing for our first sugaring season. It was a crazy addition to an already stressed schedule, but setting up to sugar was a decision Rita and I made with our family in mind. Her mother had died in November 1998 and we had invested our small inheritance from her in a piece of land in Starksboro, the town adjacent to our Bristol home. It seemed appropriate, rather than simply adding to our retirement fund, to make a commitment to the sustainable forestry movement in Vermont. Vermont Family Forests, founded by our friend David Brynn, the Addison County Forester, was attempting a comprehensive approach to this aspect of conservation and rural livelihoods in our state.

Acknowledging that Vermont has relatively little land preserved as wilderness, VFF begins by affirming the value of such public land and calling for its expansion. But the next question that arises is how to promote stewardship in the 80 percent of Vermont's forest that is in private hands. The economics of forestry have been such that landowners can often not make a sustainable profit selling logs to mills at stumpage rates. Thus, both smallholders and big commercial operators tend to clear-cut in order to realize a lump-sum profit. Often, such cutting is

71

followed quickly by subdivision and construction of second homes. Vermont Family Forests has set out to reverse this trend in two ways. The first is through landowner cooperatives that would keep the logging, milling, and drying of lumber under owners' control and boost their operations back into the black. The other is through participation in the growing "green-certification" or "smart wood" movement that is now establishing principles for sustainability in forestry. In contrast with the rapacious approach of much commercial logging, this movement is changing assumptions about acceptable practices nationwide. Vermont, with its smaller scale and vigorous dialogue about wilderness and culture, provides a laboratory for the rest of the country in this regard.

The piece of land we purchased in Starksboro was pointed out to us by our friend Lindsey Ketchel, who lives in a farmhouse across the road from it. It had been owned by a couple who wanted to subdivide it and build a cluster of upper-end homes. But the test wells they dug wouldn't support enough houses to make that proposition economically viable. The houses would have had to sell for even more if only a few could go in, and this seemed less likely because of the trailer park at the bottom of the road. David Brynn describes trailer parks as the dragons that guard Vermont's mountain treasures. It's not uncommon for them to tip the scales against the development of show homes in their vicinity. *Aji* was at work here, too.

Like many pieces of forestland in Vermont, this

one was pretty heavily logged off in the first half of the twentieth century. It will probably take several more decades of careful tending before it qualifies as a really mature northern hardwood forest. But it will still be a pleasure for us to take some of the positive actions that are already possible on it. We can mitigate erosion, for one thing, by ditching along the old logging roads and building in water bars. Cutting back the brush around old apple trees will "release" them to supply more food for various species of birds and animals. Removal of selected trees will favor faster growth and fuller crowns on the remaining maples in our sugarbush. Finally, it will be fun to map the areas of crucial habitat and the places where there are rare species in need of protection. In all these ways, we can cultivate the possibility for a diverse forest that may flourish during our children's and grandchildren's generations and beyond.

In the meantime, there are plenty of medium-size maple trees in the forest to support a sugaring operation. Caleb learned about sugaring during the semester he spent at the Mountain School, in Vershire, Vermont. The subsequent spring, he went back to help out during school vacation. Meanwhile, Matthew had been working for a construction company in Williston, gaining many of the skills that would help us out when it came time to build the actual sugarhouse. Although Rita's teaching schedule would not allow her to be as involved in the early stages of this project as our two sons and I, she enthusiastically supported our efforts and looked forward to participating in the actual sugarmaking. Our daughter, Rachel, could join us only in spirit at this first phase, having traveled to California for work the previous year after her graduation from college. We promised her the first quart of syrup. For all of us, sugaring represented an attempt to integrate the Vermont landscape more fully into the life of our family and to honor Rita's mother in a palpable way. We decided to call the stream that rushed down through the center of our property Maggie Brook, after that remarkable woman, and to call the whole operation the Maggie Brook Sugarworks.

After purchasing the property in July, we began to scout around for an appropriate spot for the sugar-house. I had my eye on a little plateau in the high, eastern part of the land, between the brook and the stateliest grove of maples on the property. I loved the thought of sitting up there in a little sugarhouse-cum-hermitage reading Bashō. The boys quickly pointed out the impracticality of this idea. It would have meant a steep hike each time we went to the sugarhouse, and thus would have made it much harder to go up repeatedly for sap collection and boiling in the midst of iffy spring weather. So we settled on a lower location, beside the main logging road and under the lee of two grand glacial erratics. Little clearing was necessary in the twelve-by-sixteen plot we laid out here—just one six-inch diameter ash had to be cut—but considerable leveling was re-quired. We unearthed many loaf-size rocks while dig-ging holes for our corner posts and door frame, and used them as a sort of foundation under the lower (western) wall. Once we had sunk and straightened the posts, we tied them together with three tiers of horizontal boards and were ready to wall in the sugarhouse with rough sawn boards from a sustainable forestry project in Bristol.

One Saturday in September, shortly after their new crop of students had arrived, Mark McKee and Alden Smith brought over a vanload of able-bodied young workers from the Mountain School to help us launch our sugarhouse. With eight people nailing boards up, the walls materialized like a large fish rising to the surface of a shady pond, or like a moose stepping forth from leaf-dappled obscurity into the bright resolution at that pond's edge. Other students dug trenches to divert runoff from the sugarhouse's eastern wall or cut up downed trees for sugar wood with their bow saws.

That got us off to a great start, generating the momentum that would carry us through the many additional tasks related to constructing the sugarhouse. Shoveling wheelbarrow after wheelbarrow of gravel over the threshold to make a floor. Forming and pouring a deeply based cement pad to support the evaporator. Laying out the rafters, including a higher cupola roof with sides that hinged down to allow steam to escape. Screwing on the corrugated metal roof, with a few translucent plastic panels to provide a little more light in this building far from any electric line. Inserting and framing up a motley collection of windows we had picked up at yard sales and salvage stores. Assembling the three-by-six-foot evaporator and lining its lower "arch" with mortared firebrick. Pushing through and framing a high metal chimney.

During the fall, Caleb had been in Namibia on a semester-long program in wildlife conservation. He was taking a year off before starting college, and had arranged his schedule to be back in time for the actual sugaring. That meant that the big fall push was basically up to Matthew and me. Many a Saturday and Sunday went into this haphazard but intensive construction effort. Often, too, I came over for an hour of work when my Middlebury College day was done, sometimes meeting him when he was coming off a long day of construction. As the days shortened and the air cooled, our sense of urgency increased. Never before have I listened so hard to the countdown of the Vermont year.

This first season of sugaring also heightened my awareness of the ironies, and the hopefulness, of a living, land-based tradition. I complained to Rita about what an enormous job this had all turned out to be—and in a fall semester that was already pretty overwhelming. And I remarked ruefully that much of the setup for sugaring had to be explained to us by those in the know, rather than involving techniques we could simply read up on. I felt this latter challenge most sharply when trying to assemble the evaporator we purchased from the Leader Company in St. Alban's. We had decided to go with a new evaporator, since only in the last few years have the pans on top been constructed with lead-free solder. All the used ones we could locate were much older than that. When our evaporator arrived, along with a load of firebricks and refractory cement, we were informed by Sam Cutting Sr. at Dakin Farm, who sold it to us, that we should use the bricks to line the arch. An arch was originally a free-standing brick or stone unit to hold the fire under the pans, but today that term simply refers to the metal firebox under the evaporator pans. It's just another vestigial word sugarmakers use and neophytes have to figure out, in the same way an intersection near Bristol might be called Daniel Four Corners after a family that no longer lives there but that everybody except a newcomer would remember. A layer of bricks is mortared onto every interior surface of the stove as well as into the long chamber running under the back half of the evaporator. The theory behind this process is a sound one, once one catches on. Bricks insulate the interior and sides of the whole system so that the heat has nowhere to go but straight up into the evaporator pans where the sap is boiled. But the walls between the stove and the air chamber that runs beneath the evaporator flare out. This makes it even harder to mortar the bricks snugly together and to avoid the gaps that would burn out the exposed sheet metal in a couple of seasons. Many a brick has to be cut in half or split into little wedges to fill those niches. I kept wondering, while pursuing my trial-and-error course of arch bricking and driving back over to Dakin Farm for advice from Sam, why the evaporator couldn't have come with more explicit instructions or, for that matter, with bricks cut to fit the required shapes.

The biggest challenge for us was figuring out how to string the lines that carried sap down to our tank from the steep eastern slope behind the sugarhouse. We decided to tap about thirty trees below and right around the sugarhouse with buckets, but in the first year we also designated about eighty more trees on the uphill side for inclusion in a pipeline system. Leader makes a full range of tubing and fittings, and Sam helped us figure out which items to order for our purposes. But even when they arrived in January and we started trying to assemble them into a system, we were basically clueless on how to proceed. My first thought was that we were suffering from the absence of written instructions. But I came to realize that our lack of any direct experience in sugaring was the more basic problem. For anyone who had seen an evaporator work or walked around the woods when sap line was being strung, the logic of the whole system would have felt self-evident. What's to explain?

Again, Sam showed us how it works. First you string a heavy-gauge wire downhill toward the sugarhouse, running approximately through the center of your sugarbush. You use special ratchets to pull this wire as taut as possible, so that when the main line is suspended on it with loops of much lighter wire, it will not sag and allow sap to freeze at the low spots. At intervals in the main line, you insert little fittings with connections for up to four branch lines. Those smaller gauge lines (blue in our case, by contrast to the main line's gray) angle upslope like fishbones joining the fish's spine. Once you've identified a row of a dozen or so trees to tap into a given branch line, you start at the farthest one out, tying a loop of branch line around it with special solid connectors. The only flow from this tree is straight down, through the short line, or "drop," that hangs from the spout where the tree is tapped. Hooking that into the end of the branch line requires a certain kind of plastic gizmo. A second sort of fitting is cut into the line each time it passes another tappable maple. Sap flows straight through the line at these points, as well as entering the line through another drop.

You have to pull each branch line taut, since there's not a supporting wire like the one for the main line. So cutting in taps along the way is a challenge calling for a special tool: you've got to cut and reattach the branch line without letting it sag. This tool makes me laugh, as the perfect embodiment of the jerry-rigged technology of sugaring. It is a gawky assemblage of parts, spray painted red in an endearing gesture at uniformity, which includes two handles loosely hinged onto an end-piece where two entirely recognizable vise grips are welded. There's also a gap in the middle of that end-piece, held together by a spring and expandable or contractable by the two handles. Attaching the vise grips on either side of where you want the drop to be cut in, you remove a segment of branch line with pruning shears, fit in a connector, press the handles together until it seats firmly into the line, release your vise grips, and move on down the line.

When I was growing up, the Sunday funnies still reprinted large-panel cartoons by Rube Goldberg depicting the most elaborate machines, complete with levers, springs, pullies, ramps, steam vents, trampolines, and parachutes to do the simplest operations. This drop cutter, like the multiple-baffled and piped evaporator pans, strikes me as a Rube Goldberg device. Something that a Vermont farmer with time on his hands between the seasons of haying and outdoor repairs might have thought up. Perfectly functional, though more ingenious than elegant. And also a lot of fun to show off and explain—mechanical marvels into which the younger generation can be elaborately initiated.

Rita helped me bring all the effort and complexity of setting up to sugar into perspective. When I was moaning one day about what an endless task this was, in a life already crowded by commitments, she responded warmly to the whole undertaking. She said she loved the energy invested in land-based activities honoring her mother, and saw the whole project as a gift to the family. Furthermore, she pointed out, the oral tradition through which sugaring is passed along is essentially a family dynamic. No book tells how to assemble an evaporator or string a sap line because it's assumed that you learned in childhood by following your parent, uncle, or grandparent around. This could scarcely be more different from my own educational experience. Books have always offered me first access to learning something new. And, with regard to doing things outdoors, as soon as I began venturing into the wilderness for high school and college backpacking trips with friends, I also moved away from my parents' sphere.

One inkling of an alternative to the wilderness ethic, with its emphasis on solitary revelations, came to me a few years earlier in a conversation at the Bread Loaf School of English. I was talking with a Yup'ik woman who was pursuing her M.A. in the summers but living with her family in a highly traditional Alaskan village in the winters. In her community, people still moved as a group to fish camp or berry camp in the appropriate seasons, still spoke Yup'ik, and enjoyed sharing the old stories. As the two of us were standing beside a Vermont barn, discussing Thoreau and the tradition of nature writing that flourishes among his descendants, Pauline remarked that she would never have imagined trying to learn about nature by going off into the woods by herself. She said that, for her people, knowledge of nature was assumed to come from following the older generation around and watching what they did.

So I try to break into the sugaring tradition through an arduous process that relies upon trial and error, as well as frequent conversations with Sam Cutting Sr. He has taken the role of my mentor—in effect my parent in this quasi-familial process—though he might be startled to hear me put it that way. But the fact is, I have been dependent on his sponsorship in many ways. He's explained each piece of equipment, even driving up to the sugarhouse for an inspection one Sunday in mid-January, before the snow got too heavy. Sam was a stranger to me before I dropped in at his store, which, in addition to selling syrup, cheese, hams, and other Vermont products, is the local distributor for Leader sugaring equipment. But from answering my questions and coming to understand the family context of our enterprise, and perhaps also from pleasure in the traditional nature of our wood-fired, gravity-fed, nonelectrified operation, he seemed to take an increasing interest in our success. Just as Rita's enthusiastic comments did, Sam's expressions of support proved very important as I was sweating to get everything set up before the sap ran. Our intent, as Rita said, has been to participate in a living rural tradition, which we had not inherited in the usual sense. Trying to enter into any tradition as an adult can be as complicated as tapping into a branch line through which sap is already flowing. When the boys and I were doing just that one day, the sap gushed onto us out of the opening. On a couple of previous occasions, I was trying to carry out such a splicing procedure by myself but didn't have my vise grips adjusted right. So one end of the line sprang free when I made the cut, and I ended up having to go all the way back up to the end tree and pull the line taut again.

One way or another, though, those fittings are all seated in now. I can stand on the slope behind the sugarhouse with Matthew and Caleb and watch the sap coursing (as the two of them exuberantly put it) down toward the old stainless steel collecting tank that a friend in Ferrisburgh gave us. We can gauge the flow by bubbles visible through the translucent tubing. At a moment like this, I feel the beginning of a family tradition that may be able to flow beyond my fumbling efforts. Both boys have met Sam and appreciate his many forms of support, but they're not so eager anymore to hear me pass along general suggestions from anyone. They've strung some line, they've boiled some sap into syrup, and they've begun to establish their own sugaring technique. They'll make their own mistakes now and seek specific advice when needed. They've assumed ownership of the process.

Caleb returned from his spring internship in Boston just in time for sugaring season, and is already planning on fitting it into his college schedule for *next* spring. Matthew recently filled out a college application of his own and, when asked about hobbies, put down sugarmaking. They see this as part of their birthright as young Vermonters, though delayed in conveyance. Since they have also become much more confident than I about operating the evaporator, I'll learn from them now. In the branch line of tradition I stand both upslope and downslope from my sons. Their knowledge and skill flows through me, strengthening my own efforts. Maybe there's a dynamic of this sort in the transmission of any rooted culture. The older generation relies on the younger, as well as the other way around. The flow of energy must go in both directions simultaneously, a vital circuit, grounded in the seasons of a family and its native place. Although this whole enterprise began since Rachel moved away from Vermont, she always seems eager for the latest news of our activities on the land. We look forward to setting her to work in the sugarhouse, too, if she can get back for a visit next time we're boiling.

When I was growing up in the Bay Area, my mother sent me back for a summer on her family's dairy farm in Louisiana so that I could learn about the way of life there while working for my namesake Uncle John. That drenching labor in the barn and fields was a revelation to this child of the suburbs. Equally memorable were the midday dinners, accompanied by pitchers of iced tea and bottles of salt tablets, with the whole extended family gathered around the table. Such experiences showed me how to work, taught me more about who my people were, and helped me feel that I had roots in that place so different from California. They both deepened and broadened my sense of identity, and I believe that they may have also contributed to my desire to participate in the rural economy of Vermont. Who knows? Maybe visits to Starksboro during sugaring season will someday serve the same purpose for the still hypothetical children of our children as that long-ago summer with Uncle John did for me.

In reflecting about Sam Cutting Sr.'s friendly mentoring role in our sugaring, I am reminded too of my *Ojiisan*, or "grandfather," in the Kyoto Go Club on Kawaramachi. I sometimes feel like an odd duck in the sugaring world back here, and an all-around clueless one in the realm of forestry. But when I wear my old Johnson wool pants and snowshoe around pulling the branch lines straight, I look more or less like my neighbors in Starksboro. In Japan, by contrast, I was hopelessly and irremediably the oddball. Looking quite conspicuous in that club of elderly Japanese men, and with only a rudimentary command of Japanese, I was so different that the first several times I went there, people preferred to ignore me altogether rather than go to the trouble of figuring out what to make of me.

The breakthrough came when one cheerful octogenarian in a beret, who also happened to be an expert Go player, began to play games with me. He offered me pointers, helped me become a familiar sight at the Go tables, and even gave me a nickname. Most of the other players had nicknames, too, like *Akachan,* or "Baby"—a distinguished, silver-haired gentleman with rosy cheeks. Mine was *Amerika Champion,* a wry monicker that acknowledged two main facts about me. I was a foreigner and I didn't play Go very well. Still, it was a nickname, and I was becoming a regular in the club. I didn't learn my sponsor's real name until our Japanese sabbatical was nearly over and I was saying good-bye to the people at the club, when he gave me his *meishi,* or business card. When he said to call him *Ojiisan,* he was taking me under his wing.

I'm sure there are many instances where tradition is still transmitted smoothly from one generation of a family to the next in stable rural communities. But there must also be plenty in which there is a certain incongruity—a gap in the line that requires filling with a gizmo of some kind. Patience is required. Also a willingness to identify imaginatively with people who may not be a namesake uncle or a grandparent in the literal sense, but who are generous enough to serve as the equivalent in our new home. We discover such surrogate families all the time in our mobile society, if we are lucky. Rita and I found this out in graduate school. We were in New England, but our parents and brothers, nieces and nephews, were in the Bay Area. Even when we managed to make it out to California for Christmas, Thanksgiving was still a holiday we needed to improvise with our grad school peers. A group of us would collect in the apartment of one of the couples, collaborate on the mysteries of turkey and stuffing—as comically elaborate in their way as any evaporator—and play the grown-ups. For almost thirty years now, we have continued getting together with two of these other families from graduate school. In this time, the children of our three clans have grown up and entered college. Our daughter, Rachel, last year, was the first to graduate, while Margaret Hunter and David Lemly will follow this year. We grad school friends have in a way become like siblings, our children like cousins, as we annually and ceremonially fill this gap in the local topography of our lives. Families may disperse, but new families can also reconvene. When the student is ready, the Zen masters declare, the teacher will appear.

And when the family is grounded, a vital lineage may be established, running both up and down the slope of generations.

The perpetuation of a land-based culture and the placement of stones in a game of Go may both be understood in relation to *aji*. A "lingering taste" is one elegant way to generalize the process of inheritance. Season by season, Go game by Go game, we practice and pass on the *katachi*, or "good shape," of openings and patterns that have proven serviceable for our predecessors. One way to talk about *aji* is to say that every group on the board is always still in play, even when it might seem cut off. When children enter adolescence, it is not uncommon for parents to discover a gap between their assumptions and those of their teenagers—a breakdown in communication that feels like the severing of a branch line. But that doesn't have to mean the vital circuit has been destroyed. It might just be that the right fitting must be seated into the gap. In some sense, our family's sugaring operation is such a fitting for us. The land is a palpable connection, a place to work together that is not so dominated by the world of talk.

This fall, while Caleb was away in Namibia, Matthew and I worked in the sleet of December to put a metal roof on the sugarhouse. Then, in what was doubtless the wrong sequence, we built and roofed a little cupola above that, with louvers that hinged down to release steam when there was boiling going on. The sheets of corrugated roofing were awkward to handle, and the eight-foot-long louvers that we had constructed from two-by-fours and two-by-sixes were awfully heavy. Matthew has become much stronger than I through all the construction work he's done over the last year, and he was always the one to hold onto a rafter with one hand while horsing a sheet of roofing or a louver around with the other. My role was as backup—the guy who steadied an end or passed along the screws and battery-operated drill as needed. With both of us lying out on the roof, our boots hooked around rafters, we often communicated by touch. Many's the time I reached over to place a handful of screws in his hand, squeezing my fist into his as the wind rattled the unfastened panels. Those moments of warm contact amid trembling exertion and gathering twilight, with nothing more needing to be said, were the essence of the whole process for me.

The preciousness of shared work was enhanced by a couple of circumstances that might have seemed negative in themselves. One was the fact that, in addition to Matthew's growing physically stronger, I had in fact gotten weaker. It wasn't two robust young comrades on that frosty roof, but one doing the bigger job while the other struggled both to help out and, simply, hold on. All this was reinforced by the chillier days and shorter afternoons of December. We were sliding into the dark time. The Vermont climate and the tradition that flows through Milton and Wordsworth into American nature writing both place a premium on fortitude, on a hope that acknowledges the inevitability of loss.

Robert Frost did not celebrate a prosperous agricultural landscape but rather chronicled with sympathy the disappearance of a farming culture in these hills. His poems enter into the unexpected openings and connections arising within a larger pattern of loss. Getting to know Frost's work in such a landscape has also deepened my sense of the literary tradition I teach at Middlebury College. Of Wordsworth in "Tintern Abbey," who can see first his youthful vitality and then even his life slipping away, but can also affirm, "for such loss, I would believe, / Abundant recompense." Of Woolf in *To the Lighthouse,* where Lily Briscoe marvels at Mrs. Ramsay's ability, in a world of transience and missed connections, to "make of the moment one of those globed, compacted things over which thought lingers and love plays."

Our sugarbush in Starksboro is halfway up what the locals promisingly call Sugar Hill. Such elevation meant we didn't get the first couple of February runs that came to the Banana Belt of Bristol. Just as well, since we were working pretty much until March to get the last branch lines strung and our filtering system worked out. Rita and I had strung the first of those lines together, working on snowshoes in the early February woods and enjoying the break from our routines. When Caleb returned from a Boston internship that he'd set up for the six weeks after Christmas, he, Matthew, and I went up to string a couple of additional ones, to tap all of the trees, and to hang buckets around the sugarhouse. The boys took special pleasure in pointing out how the sap sped through the white lines the two of them were primarily responsible for putting up, as opposed to the more sluggish action visible in our blue ones. Their complacent assessment was that the parental lines were not as taut as theirs. When your sons bound around you in the woods, laughing and calling out that your lines are sagging, you know that you've come to an Oedipal encore in the family romance.

Our first run of sap filled the two hundred-gallon stainless steel tank that Bill Scott gave us and topped up the thirty buckets a couple of times. Caleb and Matthew did all the boiling on that occasion, since it was an especially busy moment in my semester. The resulting syrup was pronounced "squisito" by Rita's comrades in Italian class when she took a sample with her one evening. A light amber color, sweet and smooth, and with a mild, nutty aftertaste. With a bit more syrup like this, we would have to develop a vocabulary like the boutique wineries in Napa County—something like "a dry oak finish, with a nose of chocolate and walnuts." As the season progresses, it's common for the syrup one makes to grow darker. Some people used to stop when they were no longer producing the velvety transparency of Grade A Fancy. But many people like ourselves liked the darker, more robust runs just as well, so most sugaring operations now produce syrup right to the end of the season. The grading system has also changed. It used to be Grade A Fancy, Grade A, Grade B, and Grade C. Now it's Grade A Fancy, Grade A Light Amber, Grade A Medium Amber, Grade A Dark Amber, and Grade B. I guess dark syrup can also be considered premium syrup now.

Several days ago, we started boiling from the second run. I drove home to Bristol from the college at around four, so that I could head up to the sugarhouse where Caleb had been boiling since about noon with his friend Devin. We'd had an intervening stretch of almost two weeks with no sap running, first because, day and night, the temperature never dropped below the freezing mark and then because of a stretch when it never rose *above* freezing. But now we were back in the zone. Suddenly our bulk tank and our buckets were overflowing, and sap was backed up in our lines. This rhythm of waiting, waiting, and then rushing around to deal with the gush makes me think of Frost's "After Apple-Picking," with its "load on load of apples coming in," and its declaration, "I am overtired / Of the great harvest I myself desired." Of Keats's "To Autumn," too, with its "season of mists and mellow fruitfulness" that swells fruit, gourd, and flower until the honeybees find that "Summer has o'erbrimm'd their clammy cells." The world's plenty is a rhythm to which we give ourselves, and when the culmination comes, there can be no holding back until the force is spent.

While I was at home changing my clothes, Matthew came in, too, having taken off early from his job with Hubbard Construction to get in on the boiling. So we threw some logs from our woodpile into the back of his truck and drove up to the sugarhouse together. Since this was the first year of our sugaring operation, we didn't get an adequate load of wood in before the snow flew. When you boil for twelve hours at a time, with a huge firebox constantly stoked up and roaring, you can go through a lot of wood in a few days. The logging road leading up to our sugarhouse was a real mud hole at this point. Matthew had to put his truck into four-wheel drive and attach his chains, and we had to labor and back up for running starts all along the way.

The sugarhouse was a beautiful sight when we arrived in the dusk. Steam was billowing out of the louvers we had so laboriously built, and a golden light from the Coleman lantern within was shining out of the open door, glowing through the panels of roofing where we'd used translucent plastic, and illuminating both the steam and the smoke from our chimney. All around this little emblem of industry were dark woods. Not a light was to be seen anywhere else. As the evening progressed, we heard a barred owl calling from farther down the slope, and right before we left some coyotes howled up on the ridge.

While the first sap run had yielded a light amber syrup, this one was producing a medium amber. In both cases, though, to get from the transparent, waterlike sap to the thick richness of syrup was a long process. The syrup feeds into the evaporator pans through a valve that is controlled by a float, designed to keep just the right amount of sap boiling so that the pans never dry out and scorch. Baffles divide the first pan, which is over the air chamber, into two long compartments that open into each other only at one end. The sap in this pan never gets very dark. But it does sweeten as it steams away, and one traditional sugarmaker's drink is to dip in a cup, then make tea with the hot sap. When Caleb was learning how to sugar at the Mountain School, he came to enjoy drinking a cup of sap tea while eating a dill pickle. The other pan, which is right over the actual stove, maintains a heavier boil and is where the syrup begins to appear. This one is divided into four long sections, open to each other only at alternate ends. From time to time the hot syrup from the final compartment is tested by filling up a narrow metal cup with it and dropping in a hydrometer, which looks like a thermometer with a weighted end. When the syrup is not quite dense enough, the hydrometer rests on the bottom of the cup. But as it continues to thicken, the hydrometer will float up little by little, until a red line is exposed and shows the requisite density has been achieved. That's when a faucet on the side of the evaporator is opened and a cup or two of syrup is drawn off into a large metal cannister with a felt filter hanging inside. This cannister has another faucet at the bottom so that, when the syrup has all filtered through, it can be decanted into our Mason jars and plastic jugs. All of the rest of the sap-syrup gradient in the evaporators moves along its sinuous bed when some is drawn off at the end, with fresh sap entering the first pan and beginning to steam toward readiness.

Standing in the sugarhouse with Matthew, Caleb, and Devin, I was enveloped in the sweet steam that hung at head level before gliding up and out the open louvers. Cracks between the vertical wallboards admitted cold March air, while occasionally we opened the door to let in even more of the evening. At one point, I went out to listen to the owls and to walk for a little way up the snowy, untracked logging road that curved into the woods. When I came back through the sugarhouse door, I smelled an aroma of caramel rising from the evaporator, then felt a jolt of heat from the stove's wide-open draft. With so much sap to boil, we tried to keep the stove full, adding a piece of wood at a time in order never to block the flames and retard the boil.

Devin, like Caleb's other close friend Mike, comes from long generations of Vermonters, for whom sugaring was once an annual ritual. But neither of those families operates a sugarhouse now, while we, the arrivals from "away," do. My sense is that these friends love coming up here to sugar in part because of its resonance with their own families. Our sons, too, take pride in participating in this ceremony of the seasons and in sharing it with their friends. There is a collaborative feeling about the process that enhances the excitement. I have never seen Matthew or Caleb more careful about any physical work. Matthew, whose room at home can scarcely be walked across without using a snow shovel on the drifts of clothing, is the most punctilious of filterers. He carefully rinses out and alternates squares of sheeting, which he holds above the felt filter bag and tilts back and forth when we draw off syrup from the evaporator. This means that the fine sludge in the evaporators never enters our containers, and the final product is beautifully transparent. Next season, Matthew has plans to insert more filters into the feed line that goes from the main line to the tank, and into the pipe from the tank to the evaporator. Caleb similarly maintains the highest of standards for this operation. He takes responsibility for the evaporator, switching the feed from side to side and cleaning out the pans between boilings. He will be in charge, too, when we clean all the equipment at the season's end. I've noticed that Caleb also shows a special interest in decorating (if that is the right word) the sugarhouse. He brought a tall wooden stool back from Namibia specifically to use while sitting reflectively by the evaporator, and he hung his prized blue-and-white Scottish flag (the traditional St. Andrew's cross design) on the sugarhouse wall. Caleb is also the one who remembers to maintain the subsidiary traditions— bringing up the pickles and the cups and tea bags, as well as his fiddle.

While a boil can have you hanging around the evaporator for twelve hours at a time and doing something to adjust the fire or draw off syrup every twenty or thirty minutes, you're generally just hanging out. There's no time to grade papers, and not even much time to read. But it's perfect for talking, for dreaming, and for listening to Caleb lift the occasional swirling fiddle tune up into the steam. As when

I worked with Matthew putting up the roof, this has proven a great time with both boys. At Middlebury College I can count on extended conversations with students in my office. But our own college-age children, not surprisingly, rarely want to settle down for a long talk with Rita and me in the living room. At the sugarhouse, though, we can all have a never-ending sequence of five-minute conversations—about family members near and far, about movies or books, about the sounds and animals and boulders and brooks of the surrounding woods. These bursts of talk add up. They are the real sugaring off from the seasons that have brought us here.

John Elder
A PORTRAIT

by Scott Slovic

Teaching is *our work!*

—John Elder

Suffused with sweetness, I turn my thoughts to one of the eloquent visionaries of my profession. I'm thinking at this moment not of environmental writing and activism, but of teaching. Mention the name John Elder in almost any crowd of environmental scholars and heads will turn. "John Elder changed my life." "I learned so much from John Elder." "St. John has a damn force field around him—such grace and gentleness and energy."

On my writing table, I've placed a small, ceramic dish of maple syrup, a portion of the first delightful batch of Vermont sweetness gathered and boiled down by John and his boys, Matthew and Caleb, in March 2000, when my own son, Jacinto, and I were passing through town. I'm not normally given to assembling totems, but this feels different. Several spoonfuls of syrup, a bear carved from thumb-size black stone (a Zuni fetish given to me by Terry Tempest Williams when my second son died), and a white, fractured rock from Jacinto, picked up at Crystal Mountain near Reno—these tokens of grace seem relevant to the occasion of reflecting on one of the magic elders of the teaching community.

There's something unusual about the sweetness of this year-old maple syrup. Although it's been sitting in an ordinary canning jar on my bookshelf for the past ten months, it has a strangely woody taste—sweetness with substance. I look at the reddish brown liquid in the nearby jar, as it takes in the clear Nevada sunlight. This is not the dark, muddy syrup I've known all my life from the neighborhood grocery store. The mere sight of it, now intensified by my first taste since standing nearly a year ago in the Elder family's hillside sugarhouse, brings to mind the twinkle in John's eye, the pleased skip in his voice, when he tasted the first syrup he and his sons had produced, clad in a plaid logger's shirt and jeans, bearded, deeply at home in Vermont.

This *credo* project is largely about words and ideas, about becoming a writer and about the writer's involvement in the intellectual and political aspects of his region's management of natural resources. Increasingly over the past decade, John Elder has become interested in the rewilding of New England, the return of forests and wildlife to the fields and hillsides that European inhabitants who arrived here in the seventeenth century and their descendants have long denuded. I initially intended to focus this portrait on Elder-qua-writer, but as I reread his books and thought more deeply about my own relationship to him, I realized that although his books and articles and lectures are invariably eloquent and provocative and cutting edge, what most powerfully characterizes John's life and work is the phenomenon of teaching and learning and his own role as teacher and learner. It seems inadequate to focus on his writing without foregrounding his teaching, and it seems inadequate to emphasize his famous teaching without pointing out his unending efforts to learn new things. Strikingly, even when teaching, even when lecturing, he often, in all sincerity and humility, adopts the perspective of fellow learner. This may be one of the keys, in fact, to the extraordinary impact he has had on the lives of students, colleagues, and friends far and wide.

I scrape the final crusts of maple syrup from the ruddy dish on my table, and an image comes to mind from the visit to Vermont last spring. One of John's responsibilities at Middlebury that semester was to sit in on classes as part of the college's assessment of teaching. He told me, though, that he hoped to see the college go beyond the current emphasis on evaluation during reviews for faculty reappointment and to institute an optional mentoring program for both teaching and scholarship. During our few days in town, trips to the sugarbush to check on Caleb's progress with the sap boiling and discussions in the office about environmental literature, college life, and the game Go were punctuated by John's rushing off to catch another colleague's class—once a biology lecture, another time a presentation on international economics. The image I'm left with, a rather comic one, is of the view from an upstairs window in Middlebury's labyrinthine new student union. John, Jacinto, and I had just eaten black bean burgers and French fries for lunch, and he left us to our crumbs while he hurried off to observe a biology lab. Jacinto and I gazed out the window at the placid, beautiful campus—gray sidewalks and stone buildings, vast lawns of yellow, late winter grass, students and professors calmly making their way to classes and meetings. And then John Elder emerged into the picture, heading away from the union, trotting across the lawn at an eagerly urgent clip, late for class, his bald pate unmistakable even from above and behind. I think of this image whenever I recall our visit to Middlebury, a token of John's eager energy, his willingness to break rank, and his incessant contribution to teaching and learning. The last crusts of syrup taste like the best part of a toasted marshmallow, the gently browned skin of a well-roasted treat.

It occurred to me that if I were going to make John's role as a teacher one of the focal points of this portrait, I should do the obvious thing: talk to some of his students. And so I did.

You don't have to look far in the community of environmental thinkers, writers, educators, and activists to find people who consider themselves students of John Elder. I suspect many who have only read his books or heard him speak at conferences would be pleased to call themselves his students as well. But I went for information to four people who have studied with John in his most recognizable teaching roles: as an English professor at Middlebury College, Vermont, since 1973, and as a faculty member at the Bread Loaf School of English (associated with Middlebury) intermittently since 1983.

I called up Laurie Lane-Zucker, managing director of the Orion Society, for some initial thoughts about John-as-teacher. Laurie had a meeting to attend in ten minutes, but he was so pleased to have an occasion to talk about John that he said: "Well, let's just get into the conversation and see where it goes. I'll postpone the meeting if I have to." Laurie was an undergraduate at Middlebury College in the mid-1980s, and John was one of two faculty members who supervised his senior thesis in 1987; several years later, in 1991, Laurie studied with John in a Bread Loaf course on southwestern literature in Santa Fe, New Mexico. I asked Laurie if he could tell me what was especially memorable about John's teaching, if he could characterize John's style of teaching, his presence in the classroom. Even before he had met Elder, Laurie knew him by reputation. "He was known as one of the most visionary professors at Middlebury, and I was aware that he was bringing the humanities to bear on thinking about people and nature. I knew that he was offering a truly original perspective on contemporary literature, and that he had the reputation as somebody who was an astonishingly good in-class leader, somebody gentle, and a very good listener." In helping Laurie with his senior thesis, Elder was particularly important in offering guidance about appropriate classic readings—Wordsworth, Tolstoy, Jung, and especially Emerson—squarely in the European and American canon and relevant to a study of "the suffusion of spirit as it manifests itself through language, story, and life" in works such as *The Prelude, Anna Karenina,* and Jung's autobiographical writings. Several years later, when Laurie finally experienced Elder in the classroom, during the Bread Loaf seminar, he was taken with the teacher's acute sensibility and strong rapport with students, with his engagement in the "spiritual dimension of nature as expressed in writing." What fascinates Laurie and other students I spoke with is how Elder manages to guide discussions without being explicitly deterministic. He seems to do so by becoming a fellow student, listening carefully to what others in a group have to say, and picking up on the strands of conversation that are relevant to the angles of thought he hopes will emerge. What students tend to sense from the beginning of a discussion, Lane-Zucker suggests, is Elder's "great generosity of spirit." And this creates a foundation for searching, energetic conversation. One of the powerful paradoxes of Elder's teaching and writing is the inevitable and central conjunction of East and West, the palpable interest in Buddhism (including American exemplars such as poet Gary Snyder), and the deep grounding in European and

American discourse and history. Lane-Zucker recalls, from class sessions and other encounters, his teacher's unusual mixture of Buddhist accommodation and Western analysis and determination.

Another important feature of Elder's relationships with students is how classroom contact occasionally evolves into important professional relationships. In the case of Lane-Zucker, he was studying with Elder in Santa Fe when he chanced upon a copy of *Orion* magazine on a newsstand, read the cover story on magic and nature by up-and-coming author David Abram, and then noticed that John Elder was on the magazine's advisory board. The next day in class, Abram himself was there, captivating the students with sleight of hand and stories. Lane-Zucker, who had previously planned to enroll in Columbia University's graduate program in film, walked into Elder's office afterward and said, "I want to work for this magazine—can you put me in contact with these people?" A phone call to Olivia Gilliam led to a meeting in New York, and before long Laurie was a central member of the *Orion* staff, helping to spin off an organization called the Orion Society from what had at first been only a magazine. The Orion Society, with the help of advisors such as Elder and many of the leading environmental thinkers of our day—Wendell Berry, Barry Lopez, David Orr, Robert Michael Pyle, Pattiann Rogers, Scott Russell Sanders, Gary Snyder, Alison Deming, Mitchell Thomashow, Terry Tempest Williams, Edward O. Wilson, Ann Zwinger, and many, many others—has become one of the major forces in contemporary American society for rethinking the relationship between human beings and the rest of the planet. Through its publications, environmental education programs, and communications and support network for grassroots environmental and community organizations throughout North America, Orion has achieved far-reaching and wholesome influence on the culture. Lane-Zucker notes, however, that few people realize John Elder's influence, his "instructive gentleness," exerted from the background of the advisory board, on the Orion Society's programs and overall direction. The result has been a powerful ripple effect throughout contemporary environmental thought and action.

For all of its successes in creating beautiful publications and influential environmental education programs, the Orion Society remains an organization known primarily to a core group of environmentally oriented educators, artists, and activists; it is a "society" still relatively marginalized within American culture. Over the years, however, John Elder has participated, and often led the way, in high-profile projects that have reached mainstream audiences. Many readers of this *credo* book will be familiar with Elder's distinguished career as both writer and editor. In 1990, before there was an Association for the Study of Literature and Environment, and before there was a well-established community of environmental writers and ecocritics, he teamed up with Cape Cod nature writer Robert Finch to edit *The Norton Book of*

Nature Writing, an anthology from one of the country's major trade publishers that would help to galvanize attention to the intersection of nature and literature. Ever sensitive to community mood, Elder responded to criticisms of the predominantly Anglo-European and male contributors to the Norton book by enlisting University of California at Berkeley scholar Hertha Wong to work with him on a multicultural anthology called *Family of Earth and Sky: Indigenous Tales of Nature from around the World,* which Beacon Press published in 1994. By this time John was already executive editor of the two-volume reference work called *American Nature Writers,* published by Scribners in 1996. This collection of eighty-two articles on seventy individual authors—from Edward Abbey to Ann Zwinger—plus a dozen broader topics, has become an indispensable guide to both professional scholars and students who want to acquaint themselves with the field of nature writing. Elder's distinguished publications have all contributed profoundly to the *teaching* of environmental literature either by making many primary texts available to teachers and students or by providing the background information about particular authors and movements necessary for teachers beginning to consider how to incorporate environmental literature into their classes.

Many teachers and students will be familiar with *The Norton Book of Nature Writing, Family of Earth and Sky,* and *American Nature Writers.* Fewer people within the community of environmental teachers and writers will have come across a small, elegant essay called "Climbing the Crests," which Elder published in the fall 1997 issue of the Modern Language Association's *ADE Bulletin,* a central periodical for administrators and faculty members in college and university English departments. This three-page article, based on Elder's presentation to an Association of Departments of English summer seminar at Boston College in 1996, lays out the essential rationale for literary scholars and teachers to be thinking about the environment. The audience was the surprisingly vast community of college-level language and literature teachers, each of whom works at any given time with dozens or hundreds of students. The potential ripple effect of these carefully chosen words was immense.

Elder begins by referring to Jay Parini's well known October 1995 *New York Times* article, "The Greening of the Humanities," which cast Elder as one of the gurus of the new ecocriticism movement. Parini made the provocative assertion, "Deconstruction is compost. Environmental studies is the academic field of the 90's." Distancing himself from Parini's playful and flamboyant representation, Elder states from the outset, "My intention is testimonial, not prescriptive." He means, with characteristic humility, to tell his own story, to offer his own perspective, not to impose "the right path" from his status as ecoliterary "guru." In particular, Elder takes pains to correct Parini's implication that Elder advocates the abolishment of English departments, stating instead, "we need to move beyond separate departments and disciplines as we have understood them over the past century."

"Climbing the Crests" makes it clear from the start that the author is a member of the same community of literature teachers he is addressing. Elder quotes the entirety of Gary Snyder's eighteen-line poem "For the Children," which begins by subtly invoking the earth's vast ecological issues and then hints at possible human salvation, if only we can manage to *"stay together / learn the flowers / go light."* Five brief paragraphs of familiar dire data follow, highlighting the issues of human population growth and global warming. At this point, Elder pivots, looks his readers in the eye, and makes the crucial connection.

> My purpose in these remarks is not to dwell on such problems. We must certainly begin by facing up to the gravity of our situation, but it's also crucial that we ask ourselves where we can go from here. . . . Can we call on the resources of our artistic, spiritual, and scientific traditions to help us guide the process and, at least to some extent, to mitigate the suffering? Can we find, as Snyder seeks to do, a beautiful and sustainable vision that will unite us in a community of effort?
>
> As teachers of English, we can participate in such an effort in several important ways. One is by identifying literary works that speak powerfully and directly to environmental issues.

He proceeds to discuss the crucial bifurcation in literary environmentalism between the Western canon, ranging from Shakespeare to Terry Tempest Williams, and the world's other traditions of powerful thinking about the relation between people and planet. Somehow these cultural rifts must be bridged, and it's the appropriate role of literary scholars and teachers to see past the boundaries of language, history, and geography. Operating in testimonial mode, Elder offers, "I have found, for instance, that the Japanese poet Bashō has a remarkable affinity both with the Thoreauvian tradition and with poets in the school of Wordsworth." In other words, he argues for the combined scrutiny of Anglo-European "nature writing," Western literature without an explicit environmental focus, and non-Western literatures. References to Milton, T. S. Eliot, E. M. Forster, and Charles Dickens follow before Elder moves toward his concluding comments about Leslie Marmon Silko's inclusive, Pueblo view of the earth and its inhabitants and returns to Snyder's suggestion that the sustainable way to live is to keep in mind community ("stay together"), place-based knowledge ("learn the flowers"), and moderate impact ("go light").

What's remarkable about this essay is the acuity with which it addresses Elder's primary audience of college English professors and administrators. Even the elegance of the speaker's invocation of a notable text (the Snyder poem) and his weaving of the poem throughout the essay, following the actual structure of Snyder's work, is likely to appeal to readers' sense of order and interest in literary commentary. The references to authors range from recognizable nature writers to canonical European and American literary figures to Asian and Native American authors, supporting Elder's central claim that we must not exclude any cultural traditions from our investigation of how literature can lead us toward better understanding of our own nature and the nature of our environmental predicament. Rather than pontificating as "ecocritical guru" to nonenvironmental literati, Elder welcomes his audience as important collaborators with common skills.

> One function of English and of the other humanistic studies is to prevent narrowly technological approaches to our pressing environmental problems. Such "technofixes," to which many scientists and policy makers are drawn, have two main problems. One is that they often rely on a naive faith rather than a concrete program. . . . The other is that they locate our problems outside ourselves. But the environmental crisis is ultimately nothing other than ourselves. The discipline of English has been defined as a mode of reading that recognizes a primary value in the text itself, that assumes style to be integral to a text's meaning, and that includes the reader's experience as an important element of that meaning. This kind of reading involves the whole person— the senses and the memory as well as the mind's analytical powers. It offers a practice of

engaging with complexity that can be of great
value as our colleges and universities strive to
respond to the environmental crisis.

Readers of this statement, most of whom are likely to
be fellow English faculty members, find themselves
enlisted in Elder's cause, not castigated for their possible indifference or opposition. This is a masterful
example of teacherly rhetoric, hovering carefully between the promised "testimonial" and what comes
to sound quite a bit like advocacy if not outright
"prescription." The value of highlighting Elder's relatively little known essay, "Climbing the Crests," in
this portrait is that it illustrates how John has been
active in advancing the efficacy of environmental literature and ecocriticism well beyond his own classroom activities and his production of invaluable
textbooks and scholarly guides. He has encouraged
other scholars and teachers to rethink the relevance
of literature to the natural world (or to think this
through for a first time). He has urged members of
English departments to consider the value of collabo-
rating beyond the ranks of their disciplines and departments. He has even proposed such alternative
pedagogical models as "field courses" (what he calls
"teaching modes that carry me and my students back
out under the sky").

John Elder's own most notable contribution to the
field of environmental literature may be his 1998
book *Reading the Mountains of Home,* a vibrant example

of what I like to call "narrative scholarship," a style of academic writing that mixes textual commentary (or other sorts of "scholarly" reflection) with the author's stories about living in the world and about being human. Initial hints of Elder's interest in this approach to scholarly writing appeared in his first book, *Imagining the Earth: Poetry and the Vision of Nature*. This book includes two short "excursions"—titled "Hitching a Ride with the Cumberland Beggar" and "Winter without Snow"—amid critical studies of William Wordsworth, Gary Snyder, Wendell Berry, Robert Pack, Annie Dillard, Peter Matthiessen, and others. The first narrative interlude emphasizes the phenomenon of community and the role of the outsider (Wordworth's Cumberland beggar or a Middlebury English professor hitching a ride home after teaching a poetry class). The second emphasizes the relationship between the mind and the senses, suggesting that our physical experience of nature provides a crucial foundation for our *thinking* about the world. *Reading the Mountains of Home* radically expands the subtle narrative gestures of *Imagining the Earth,* subsuming and absorbing the scholarly information and analysis within a series of personal stories. As Elder points out in the introduction to *Reading,* "This book's narrative structure and voice differentiate it from literary criticism in the usual sense of the term. . . . My goal has been to explore, in a direct and personal way, an ecosystem of meaning that includes both literature and the land. What a reader will find here are thus the stories of one year's excursions through the mountains where a beloved poem is rooted, and where my family and I also live." On one level, *Reading the Mountains of Home* is an extended gloss on Robert Frost's famous 1946 poem "Directive." On another level, it's a synthetic history of New England culture and ecology, telling stories of settlement and migration, natural resource extraction, geology, and forest succession. And on yet another level, a poignant narrative stratum of family and self, the book recounts a period in the author's life during which his children have reached adolescence and are struggling to find their paths in life and his aging parents succumb to mortal frailty. The writer, despite his desire to care for his family and his adopted place, finds himself forced to accommodate, and to try to understand, the uncontrollable drama of human beings and the physical world. Much like Peter Matthiessen in *The Snow Leopard,* Elder must learn to let go. In one passage Matthiessen writes: "If the snow leopard should manifest itself, then I am ready to see the snow leopard. If not, then somehow (and I don't understand this instinct, even now) I am not ready to perceive it . . . ; and in the not-seeing, I am content."

In its opening presentation of Frost's poem, followed by the ornate-yet-accessible interweaving of anecdote, environmental and cultural history, and explications/applications of small sections of the central poem, *Reading the Mountains of Home* resembles the overarching structure of "Climbing the Crests." Some might describe it as a homiletic pattern, the architecture of a sermon, but in Elder's quiet prose, prescription and "directive" become "testimony."

In early March 2000, I lay in bed in the Elder family's comfortable, well-worn Victorian house just a stone's throw from the center of Bristol, a hamlet that closely approximates my image of the movie-set New England village. The oldest part of the house, dating back to 1820, was actually lifted up and placed atop a new living room at one point. Jacinto and I planned to join John for one of his favorite hikes in the morning. As Jacinto snored on the mattress placed on the floor, I "studied" to be ready for the hike. The plan was to walk up to the Ledges, the cliffs on North Mountain known more formally as the Bristol Ledges. John devotes an entire chapter in *Reading the Mountains of Home* to this particular place, a mountain perch that rises abruptly a quarter mile from his house and looks out over Bristol and much of western Vermont. John opens the chapter by recounting an April 1995 hike up to the Ledges with his wife, Rita, after dinner, their three teenage children remaining below at the house. As they pitched their tent to spend the night there, he writes, "The sky's last golden light gleamed on [our home's] slate roof, and there was neither a fire truck nor an ambulance in the driveway." Without fanfare or breast-beating, this gentle statement of concern expresses a father's trauma in letting go, in allowing his children to become themselves—he still watches and waits, perched on his ledge, ready to help if necessary, but forcing himself to step back. I paused now and then as I read to glance at twelve-year-old Jacinto, sprawled on the floor of the bedroom. I listened to his breathing.

One of the most memorable passages in "The Ledges" describes an event that took place there in the summer of 1982. As John and Rita drifted into sleep on the ledge, he recollected a forest fire at the same spot a dozen years before. It had permanently "changed [his] perspective on the tough boys who hang around the Green" in the center of town. By the time Elder and other men were returning home from work in the late afternoon of that day, the Bristol Fire Department had contained much of the wildfire. But, as he recalls in *Reading the Mountains of Home,*

> the flames were still roaring right below the rock, where the cliff dropped straight down toward the elementary school. And that's where the hard boys from the Green were doing their own work. There was a strip of oaks separated by just a few feet from the more continuously wooded face below, and just beginning to take flame in their upper branches. The young men lowered each other down on ropes to lop off the burning tops and prevent the fire from descending to the village. These skinny 20-year-olds in black jeans and white tee shirts, with their tattooed forearms and their faces that had rarely shown the town anything other than a scowl or snarl, were smiling and laughing as they swung through the smoke. Gripping the ropes with one hand and their keening chainsaws in the

other, they dropped toward the fire and did the town's most dangerous work.

What does it take to make a community? How to bring everybody into a meaningful, and if possible *joyful,* role? What might become of his children, and his neighbors' children, if they feel themselves shut off and disenfranchised? Such questions are embedded in the scene describing the fire and the rough kids from the Green. The college professor learns from his contemplation of the memory that "danger made these young men feel alive, and useful, up in the mountains where adventures were still possible. After listless days when they felt left behind by the purposeful traffic of North Street, they remembered in swinging below the Ledges what it felt like to *play.*" Some people like danger, even need it—and everyone needs a sense of purpose and a sense of play. The mountains near Bristol, so close to town, offer adventure and ideas to the whole community, their value sometimes buried in historical events or in information painstakingly accrued through research and conversation.

I dwell on this passage from *Reading the Mountains of Home* not only because it helps me to characterize Elder's approach in this compelling project but because it was brought to mind again recently when I was interviewing another of John's former students, Lilace Mellin Guignard. Lilace studied with Elder twice in the 1990s, first during the Orion Institute at the Bread Loaf School of English in the summer of 1996 and then again at Bread Loaf's Alaska Institute in June 1998. After telling me about Elder's "completely Zen" approach to guiding class discussions—"in the sense that he's completely humble . . . an invisible facilitator"—she recalled his visit in October 1997 to speak to her high school students at the Outdoor Academy of the Southern Appalachians, in Pisgah Forest, North Carolina. He read the passage about the tough guys from the Bristol Green to the students. Then he asked them to do some writing, first thinking about a special place where each had experienced a hard time or a loss of some kind, and then writing about "home," offering whatever memories or images that term conjured up. Just as he went out of his way in his essay for the *ADE Bulletin* to find appropriate texts and rhetorical devices to appeal to his audience of college professors, he selected an approach for his Outdoor Academy presentation that seemed well suited to his listeners. He talked to the kids about the importance of joining experience with reflection, Lilace recalled. "'Writing today has become too much of an indoor sport,' he told them. And then he talked about walking and writing, how the two go together, like the left foot and the right foot."

Lilace's husband, Jimmy, who also studied with Elder and nature writer Richard Nelson at the 1998 Alaska Institute, sat down with us. Both are now graduate students at the University of Nevada, where I work, so I've come to their house this morning to listen to stories of Bread Loaf. They paged through their journals from the 1998 field course—detailed, daily records of sights and readings and conversations, complemented with awkward sketches and with John Elder's written responses. Lilace quoted a line of Elder's from a group discussion: "Some people get very uneasy when they're lost." The implication seems to be that Elder himself is strangely comfortable when he's in new intellectual or geographical territory—when you're lost, that's when interesting things happen. "Controlling risks doesn't make sense to him," she commented, noting one of his favorite aphorisms by composition theorist Peter Elbow: "Digression is insight."

Jimmy checked his notebook to corroborate a particular instance on Alaska's Kruzof Island when Elder's own pedagogical openness was tested. One day, having worked hard to assemble the eighteen students for a discussion, John was just about to begin talking when a student came running over and exclaimed that a huge marine worm had just washed up on the nearby beach. The students peeled away from the group, leaving Elder with his books. Finally, he said to the few remaining students, "I think a marine worm trumps anything I have to say" and went to join the worm watchers. Remembering that experience, Jimmy commented, "John really opens things up for you. It's easy to be comfortable with your ideas around him. Someone who allows himself to be 'trumped by a marine worm' doesn't think he has all the answers, and he doesn't expect you to have all the answers, either." Still, it's clear from our conversation that these two students, one a poet and the other a scholar of Victorian environmental literature, both aiming for careers as writers and teachers, feel profound respect for their former teacher, acknowledging the subtle influence Elder has exerted on their lives, their views of the world, their future plans. The bound and weathered notebooks from Alaska are full of treasures.

John Clark Elder was born on March 22, 1947, in Louisville, Kentucky. His father, James Lyn Elder, was a Baptist minister and seminary professor; Bernie Lois Green, his mother, worked as a high school Latin teacher. John's only sibling, his older brother Harold Lyn Elder, became a musician and instrument maker and now lives in Petaluma, California.

The Elder family moved several times when John was a boy, following his father's church positions. They went to Richmond, Virginia, in 1948, relocating to New Orleans two years later. When John was six, his family moved to Albany, California, and his father took a teaching position at the Golden Gate Baptist Seminary. When the seminary moved across the San Francisco Bay to Marin County, the Elders moved to Mill Valley, where John spent his teenage years. He recalls his fifteenth birthday, when he received a copy of *Walden* from his parents, as a landmark moment in his youth.

His main activities as a student at Tamalpais Union High School in Mill Valley were wrestling, cross-country running, and playing the French horn.

A lanky teenager at six-feet-two and 140 pounds, he tended to have good leverage against his wrestling opponents. As he prepared to graduate in 1965, he gave serious consideration to a musical career. Instead, having received a National Merit Scholarship, he took a scholarly path and enrolled at Pomona College in southern California. Even today, though, one notices Elder's continuing interest in music; an entire room at the family home in Bristol, Vermont, is devoted to musical instruments, as his son Caleb showed me and Jacinto during our visit. His students, too, note that John loves to sing. During camping trips he invariably gets the whole group singing together.

Elder graduated from Pomona in 1969 with a B.A. in English. From there, supported by a Danforth Fellowship, he proceeded to the Ph.D. program in English at Yale University, eventually completing a dissertation called "Towards a New Objectivity: Essays on the Body and Nature in Lawrence, Faulkner, and Mann" in 1973 under the direction of Charles Feidelson Jr. He recounts some of the stresses and frustrations of graduate school in this *credo* essay, indicating how his own views of literature and pedagogy were, to some degree, shaped by his experience at Yale. In the midst of his graduate program, Elder received a Watson Fellowship, which enabled him to travel in Africa and study connections between oral and written literature. While at Yale, he also married Rita Lenore Pinkston, who had attended Pomona with him, graduating in 1970; in addition to raising the three Elder children, Rita works as a special education teacher (currently at Lincoln Community School in Lincoln, Vermont) and is a pianist and a community arts activist.

John joined the English department at Middlebury College as an assistant professor in 1973. He took leave from Middlebury to serve as director of the Thomas J. Watson Fellowship Program from 1977 to 1979. Based in Providence, Rhode Island, the travel fellowships are awarded to graduates of liberal arts colleges; former fellows serve two-year stints directing the program. During the late 1970s Elder was also introduced to contemporary American environmental literature. He encountered such recently published works as Annie Dillard's *Pilgrim at Tinker Creek* and Wendell Berry's *A Continuous Harmony.* John and Rita also began their family; Rachel was born in 1977, followed by Matthew in 1980 and Caleb in 1981.

A fellowship from the National Endowment for the Humanities enabled the Elders to spend 1980–81 at the University of California at Berkeley, where John wrote his first book, *Imagining the Earth: Poetry and the Vision of Nature.* This book appeared in 1985 from the University of Illinois Press and was reissued in 1996 by the University of Georgia Press, in response to the emergence of a new audience of ecological literary critics and teachers of environmental literature since the mid-eighties. It was during the year at Berkeley that Elder also began his study of Zen Buddhism.

In 1981, newly tenured at Middlebury and

promoted to associate professor, John began his regular summer teaching for the Bread Loaf School of English, a graduate program associated with Middlebury. Over the coming years, he offered through Bread Loaf seminars in American nature writing and various aspects of the pastoral tradition, workshops in nonfiction nature writing, and interdisciplinary, field-based courses connecting literature and natural history. From 1982 to 1988, Elder developed courses in American nature writing and the literature of wilderness for Middlebury undergraduates. One of his first forays into the genre of scholarly writing that would later be called "ecocriticism" was the 1981 essay titled "John Muir and the Literature of Wilderness," which appeared in the *Massachusetts Review*. In the mid-eighties, he began participating in Middlebury's Environmental Studies Program, established connections with *Orion* magazine, and collaborated with Robert Finch on *The Norton Book of Nature Writing*, which appeared in 1990. A revised, expanded edition of the Norton collection appeared in 2001.

Elder was promoted to full professor in 1987. Building on his interest in Zen and Japanese culture, he began studying Japanese language at Middlebury in 1988, preparing for a 1990–91 sabbatical year in Kyoto. Prior to the year in Japan, he also began working on *Family of Earth and Sky: Indigenous Tales of Nature from around the World* with Berkeley scholar Hertha Wong. In addition, he began serving as series editor of Beacon Press's Concord Library in 1988.

During the year in Kyoto, while guiding and recording the family's adventures, John studied classical Japanese calligraphy and the game of Go. He also wrote an initial draft of *Following the Brush: An American Encounter with Classical Japanese Culture,* publishing it with Beacon in 1993.

Upon his return from Kyoto, John assumed a split appointment as professor of English and environmental studies, actually serving as director of Middlebury's Environmental Studies Program from 1991 to 1994. Having helped to organize a four-day symposium entitled "Spirit and Nature: Religion, Ethics, and the Environmental Crisis" in 1990, John coedited *Spirit and Nature,* the book that emerged from the meeting, with Middlebury colleague Steven C. Rockefeller. *Spirit and Nature,* published by Beacon Press in 1992, included articles by Jewish, Islamic, Buddhist, and several Christian leaders (the Buddhist contributor was none other than Tenzin Gyatso, His Holiness the Fourteenth Dalai Lama).

During the 1990s, while coordinating the *American Nature Writers* reference books for Scribner, working on *Reading the Mountains of Home,* and teaching English and interdisciplinary environmental studies courses at Middlebury, John also took on numerous advisory and leadership roles. He served on the editorial advisory board for *Orion* magazine from 1990 to 1996 and the advisory board for the Orion Society from 1992 to 1996, joining the society's board of directors from 1997 to 2000. He also directed Orion's "Stories in the Land" environmental education program with a grant from the Geraldine R. Dodge Foundation. At the same time, he became a founder and affiliate of the Weybridge House co-op for Middlebury students interested in environmental issues and sustainable living and joined the boards of the Vermont Land Trust and the Association for the Study of Literature and Environment. More locally, he served as founding president of the Bristol Watershed Center, a community-based conservation project. His summers were typically devoted, in part, to Bread Loaf teaching, either in Santa Fe, New Mexico, or at the Vermont campus.

By 1997, apart from summer excursions to Alaska to offer Bread Loaf field courses with nature writer Richard Nelson, Elder had become particularly focused on the study of wilderness and culture in New England, spending much of his time exploring the landscape around his home in Bristol. His major book, *Reading the Mountains of Home,* appeared in 1998 to the acclaim of both nature writers and literary scholars. It's difficult to imagine a more organic, heartfelt combination of vigorous stories of family and place and literary-ecological knowledge. In the late 1990s, Elder found himself participating regularly in regional and national meetings devoted to environmental education and conservation in Vermont, often as the keynote lecturer. One such presentation in June 1998 was at the opening ceremony at the Marsh-Billings National Historical Park in Woodstock, Vermont. A particularly rewarding personal adventure was the purchase several years ago of approximately 142 acres of maple forest in the mountains half an hour north of Bristol for the purpose of trying to practice sustainable forestry; the Elder family's "sugarbush" is where Matthew, Caleb, and he constructed a small, traditional cottage a year and a half ago and rigged the special stove for boiling sap.

John and Rita spent most of the 2000–2001 academic year on sabbatical in Europe. He received a Fulbright Research Fellowship to study the Italian phase of the career of Vermonter George Perkins Marsh, America's first minister to Italy and author of the 1864 book *Man and Nature*. A century later, this publication had a significant influence on the Wilderness Act and the establishment of the Environmental Protection Agency. Following a walk across England and France, the Elders spent six months living in Tuscany. Although the year appeared to be a respite from the academic pressures of Middlebury College and even from the familiar landscapes of New England, John's latest writing project has everything to do with the landscape and ideas that have come to occupy his time in recent years. As he put it in his Fulbright application statement, Elder planned to work on a book project that, taking its "cue" from Marsh, aimed to "evoke the *ecology* of environmental thought: a system that encompasses both wild lands and working landscapes, that values the voices of long-settled terrain like Vermont and Tuscany, and that seeks to strike a fresh balance through the venerable but timely ideal of stewardship." He has already published on the Vermont aspects of these themes in such articles as "Inheriting Mt. Tom" and "A Conversation at the Edge of Wilderness."

When I was visiting Middlebury in the spring of 2000, John mentioned in passing his standard, silent retort to professorial colleagues who express their eagerness for the beginning of summer, when they can finally get back to their "work": "Teaching *is* our work!" I had this in mind as I reread *Following the Brush* a few months ago, looking for a way into the author's life and work. The book's first full chapter, also called "Following the Brush," is ostensibly about calligraphy and the struggles of an American neophyte to learn this classical Japanese art form. I had read the book in preparation for my own Fulbright in Japan in 1993–94, but at that time I had not dwelled upon the possible metaphoric implications of the calligraphy chapter, instead looking for survival tips. How might an American get by in such an exotic culture? This time through, it struck me that much of the book is concerned with processes of teaching and learning. What's particularly interesting is how the experienced, nay venerated, professor plays the role of learner in this text. When he realizes the meaning of his Kyoto calligraphy teacher's indirect, non-explanatory method of demonstrating brushstrokes, he writes, "Through his nondirective teaching he bestowed a practice centered in looking and doing, not in thinking, and released me from the analytical nexus that so easily turns impulses into calculations." In an ironically vivid, self-expressive way,

Elder proceeds to comment appreciatively on the virtues of this rather different approach to teaching and learning: "After an American education in the liberal arts, where a high value is placed upon self-expression and originality, I was just beginning to glimpse the value, and the challenge, of imitation." By losing himself in the wilderness of a new art form, a new language, and a new culture, the master teacher presses himself into the role of learner—and the mind opens yet further.

When it occurred to me that *Following the Brush* was primarily a study of teaching and learning, I began to see the teaching process as central to all of John Elder's work, not only in his engagement with students of various kinds but in his writing as well. A few weeks later, I called Jennifer Sahn, managing editor of *Orion Afield* and a student of John's at Middlebury in the early 1990s, to see if this idea made sense to her. She told me the story of her own experiences as John's student: her three-year quest to take his famous class called "Visions of Nature" (required for environmental studies majors), her pitching a senior thesis topic on experiential education to him, her request that he supervise her student-teaching project, and his response—"Well, this all sounds very exciting." She described his method of listening carefully while still guiding class discussions: "It's like he's patting his head and rubbing his belly at the same time, the way he follows the organic connections in conversation." Patting his head and rubbing his belly. I like that image of the listener and discussion leader, the teacher and writer, inspiring other minds and at the same time teasing and challenging his own intellect. "His approach in class discussions is to advance ideas as part of a learning community," Jennifer continued, "so that everyone comes out feeling like their ideas have shifted. And his lectures, too, are thrilling. I remember leaving class, when I was taking 'Visions of Nature,' feeling like I was walking on air. He would range far off on tangents and then tie everything together by the end."

Lecturing, listening, patting his head and rubbing his belly, inspiring his students and his readers to think for themselves, to walk on air. I think of this man of varied interests and powerful focus—Baptist by birth and Buddhist by study, raised in the beige hills of Marin County and now at home in the maple forests of Vermont, a lover of people and a fan of wildness. What more will John Elder accomplish as he turns the corner and enters the final phase, the "frog run," of his career? Some of his plans are forecast in this *credo* essay, but if a giant marine worm washes ashore, these plans may simply be cast away.

Bibliography of John Elder's Work

by Lilace Mellin Guignard

BOOKS

Reading the Mountains of Home. Cambridge: Harvard University Press, 1998. Cambridge: Harvard University Press, 1999.

Following the Brush: An American Encounter with Classical Japanese Culture. Boston: Beacon Press, 1993. Boston: Beacon Press, 1994. Reprint ed. Pleasantville, N.Y.: Akadine Press, 1999. Tokyo: Bunjinsha, forthcoming.

With Dixie Goswami, Betsy Bowen, and Jeffrey Schwartz. *Word Processing in a Community of Writers*. New York: Garland Publishing, 1989.

Imagining the Earth: Poetry and the Vision of Nature. Urbana: University of Illinois Press, 1985. Athens: University of Georgia Press, 1996.

EDITED BOOKS

The Return of the Wolf: Reflections on the Future of Wolves in the Northeast. Hanover, N.H.: University Press of New England, 2000.

American Nature Writers: Edward Abbey to John McPhee. Vol. 1. New York: Charles Scribner's Sons, 1996.

American Nature Writers: Peter Matthiessen to Western Geologists and Explorers. Vol. 2. New York: Charles Scribner's Sons, 1996.

With Hertha Wong. *Family of Earth and Sky: Indigenous Tales of Nature from Around the World.* Boston: Beacon Press, 1994. Boston: Beacon Press, 1996.

With Steven Rockefeller. *Spirit and Nature: Why the Environment Is a Religious Issue—An Interfaith Dialogue.* Boston: Beacon Press, 1992.

With Robert Finch. *The Norton Book of Nature Writing.* New York: W. W. Norton, 1990. 2nd ed. New York: W. W. Norton, 2001.

UNCOLLECTED ESSAYS AND CRITICISM

"Forever Wild Again: A Walk Toward Romance Mountain." Published for the campaign of the Vermont Wilderness Association, Summer 2001.

"The Poetry of Experience." *New Literary History* 30, no. 3 (Summer 1999).

"A Conversation at the Edge of Wilderness." *Wild Earth* 8, no. 4 (Winter 1998/1999): 30–34.

"Fragments of Vanished Lives." *Whole Terrain* 7 (Winter 1998/1999): 15–19.

"Rendezvous at Dead Creek." *Yankee Magazine* 62, no. 11 (November 1998): 35–36.

"Teaching at the Edge." *Orion Afield* 2, no. 1 (Winter 1997/1998): 42–43.

"Climbing the Crests: An Environmental Approach to Literature." *Associated Departments of English Bulletin,* no. 117 (Autumn 1997): 27–30.

"Inheriting Mt. Tom." *Orion* 16, no. 2 (Spring 1997): 27–32.

"The Turtle in the Leaves." *Orion* 13, no. 1 (Winter 1994): 24–25.

"Mary Oliver's Question." *American Nature Writing Newsletter* 5, no. 2 (Fall 1993): 10–11.

"North Mountain Gyres." *Orion* 11, no. 3 (Summer 1992): 38–42.

"Hiking Off the Trail: One Teacher's Approach to Nature Writing." *CEA Critic* 54, no. 1 (Autumn 1991): 19–21.

"Gyres Above North Mountain: What the Return of the Peregrine Falcon Will Tell Us—If We Listen." *Vermont Life* 46, no. 1 (Autumn 1991): 26–29.

Review of *Practice of the Wild,* by Gary Snyder. *Orion* 10, no. 1 (Winter 1991): 59.

"Wilderness and Walls." *Orion* 8, no. 4 (Autumn 1989): 28–35.

With Kathleen Skubikowski. "Word Processing in a Community of Writers." *College Composition and Communication* 38, no. 2 (May 1987): 198–201.

Editorial. *Orion* 6, no. 1 (Winter 1987): 3.

"Hunting in Sand County." *Orion* 5, no. 4 (Autumn 1986): 46–53.

Editorial. *Orion* 5, no. 1 (Winter 1986): 3.

"Vermonters and Wilderness: A Legacy and a Lesson." *Vermont Life* 39, no. 1 (Autumn 1984): 48–55.

Review of *W. H. Hudson: A Biography,* by Ruth Tomalin. *Orion* 3, no. 2 (Spring 1984): 56–57.

"John Muir, Ansel Adams, and the Range of Light." *Orion* 3, no. 1 (Winter 1984): 12–19.

Review of *I-Mary,* by Augusta Fink, and *The Land of Journeys' Ending,* by Mary Austin. *Orion* 2, no. 4 (Autumn 1983): 50–51.

"Seeing Through the Fire: Writers in the Nuclear Age." *New England Review and Bread Loaf Quarterly* 5, no. 4 (Summer 1983): 647–54.

"John Muir and the Literature of the Wilderness." *Orion* 2, no. 2 (Spring 1983): 24–33.

"The Natural History of American Culture." *New England Review* 4, no. 1 (Autumn 1981): 152–57.

"John Muir and the Literature of the Wilderness." *Massachusetts Review* 22, no. 2 (Summer 1981): 375–86.

Review of *Speaking for Nature,* by Paul Brooks, and *A Species of Eternity,* by J. Kastner. *New England Review* 4, no. 1 (Autumn 1981): 152–64.

"Winter Without Snow: Literature and Attitudes to Environment." *New England Review* 3, no. 2 (Winter 1980): 161–69.

BOOK INTRODUCTIONS AND FOREWORDS

Foreword to *The Height of Our Mountains: Nature Writing from Virginia's Blue Ridge Mountains and Shenandoah Valley,* edited by Michael P. Branch and Daniel J. Philippon. Baltimore: John Hopkins University Press, 1998.

"Teaching at the Edge." Introduction to *Stories in the Land: A Place-Based Environmental Education Anthology.* Great Barrington, Mass.: Orion Society, 1998.

"Sauntering Toward the Holy Land." Introduction to *Nature,* by Ralph Waldo Emerson, and *Walking,* by Henry David Thoreau. Illustrated ed., Boston: Beacon Press, 1991. Boston: Beacon Press, 1994.

With Steven C. Rockefeller. Introduction to *Spirit and Nature: Visions of Interdependence* (exhibition catalog). Middlebury, Vt.: Christian A. Johnson Memorial Gallery, Middlebury College, 1990.

ANTHOLOGY APPEARANCES

"The Poetry of Experience." In *Beyond Nature Writing,* edited by Kathleen R. Wallace and Karla Armbruster. Charlottesville: University Press of Virginia, 2001.

With Christopher McGrory Klyza, Jim Northup, and Stephen Trombulak. "Connecting with Human and

Natural Communities at Middlebury College." In *Acting
Locally: Concepts and Models for Service-Learning in
Environmental Studies,* edited by Harold Ward.
Washington, D.C.: American Association for Higher
Education, 1999.

"Education in a Time of Environmental Crisis." In
Population and Environment, edited by Barbara Baudot
and William Moomaw. Basingstoke, England:
Macmillan, 1997.

"Development and a Candle." In *Ethical and Spiritual
Dimensions of Social Progress.* New York: United Nations
Publication, 1995.

"Wildness and Walls." In *Worldly Words: An Anthology of
American Nature Writing,* edited by Scott Slovic. Tokyo,
Japan: Fumikura, 1995.

"The Plane at South Mountain." In *Being in the World:
An Environmental Reader for Writers,* edited by Scott H.
Slovic and Terrell F. Dixon. New York: Macmillan,
1993.

"'Brightened for the Passage': Nature's Refrain in American
Poetry." In *Columbia History of American Poetry,* edited
by Jay Parini and Brett Millier. New York: Columbia
University Press, 1993.

"Wildness and Walls." In *Finding Home,* edited by Peter
Sauer. Boston: Beacon Press, 1992.

With Kathleen Skubikowski. "Computer Networks
and the Social Context of Writing." In *Computers
and Community,* edited by Carolyn Handa. Boston:
Heinemann Publishing/Boynton-Cook, 1990.

"The Plane at South Mountain." In *Bread Loaf Anthology
of Contemporary American Essays,* edited by Robert Pack
and Jay Parini. Hanover, N.H.: University Press of New
England, 1989.

"Seeing Through the Fire." In *Writing in a Nuclear Age,*
edited by Jim Schley. Hanover, N.H.: University Press
of New England, 1984.

INTERVIEWS

"A Human Place in the Wilderness: A Conversation with
    John Elder." *American Hiker* 12, no. 4 (August/September
    1999): 12, 16.
"In Pursuit of a Bioregional Curriculum: An Interview with
    John Elder." Interview by Jennifer Sahn. *Orion Afield* 3,
    no. 2 (Spring 1999): 26–28.

BIOGRAPHICAL/CRITICAL STUDIES AND REVIEWS

Ackerman, Diane. "Nature Writers: A Species unto
    Themselves." Review of *The Norton Book of Nature
    Writing. New York Times Book Review* (May 13, 1990):
    1, 42.
Bach, Pamela L. Review of *American Nature Writers. RQ* 36,
    no. 4 (Summer 1997): 594.
Barnett, Adrian. Review of *Reading the Mountains of Home.
    New Scientist* 158, no. 2138 (June 13, 1998): 47–49.
Bibel, Barbara. Review of *American Nature Writers. Booklist*
    93, no. 11 (February 1, 1997): 961–62.
Bohjalian, Chris. "The Wilderness Around Us." *Boston
    Globe Magazine* (April 12, 1998): 12, 27–32.
Borrelli, Peter. Review of *Reading the Mountains of Home.
    Amicus Journal* 20, no. 3 (Fall 1998): 40–41.
Bouma-Predigen, Steven. Review of *Spirit and Nature.
    Journal of Religion* 73, no. 2 (April 1993): 276–78.
Buchanan, W. C. Review of *Imagining the Earth. Choice* 23,
    no. 6 (February 1986): 867.
Carpenter, Richard P. "A Warm View of Japan—and a
    Wacky One." Review of *Following the Brush. Boston
    Globe* (February 7, 1993): B44.
Coeyman, Marjorie. "For These Students, Writing Comes
    Naturally." *Christian Science Monitor* (April 28, 1998): B3.
Craft, Carolyn. Review of *Spirit and Nature. Library Journal*
    117, no. 8 (May 1, 1992): 88.

Curwen, Thomas. "Exploring Robert Frost's Last Great Poem." Review of *Reading the Mountains of Home. Los Angeles Times* (April 10, 1998): E8.

Deeley, Mary. Review of *Spirit and Nature. Booklist* 88, no. 19 (June 1, 1992): 1734–35.

Donavin, Denise Perry. Review of *Following the Brush. Booklist* 89, no. 8 (Dec. 15, 1992): 710.

Dykhuis, Randy. Review of *Reading the Mountains of Home. Library Journal* 123, no. 5 (March 15, 1998): 90.

Elbers, Joan S. Review of *Family of Earth and Sky. Library Journal* 119, no. 13 (August 1994): 94.

"Elder, John." *Contemporary Authors.* New Revision Series, vol. 82, 111–12. Detroit: Gale Group, 2000.

Flower, Dean. "Nature Does Not Exist for Us." Review of *Reading the Mountains of Home. Hudson Review* 52, no. 2 (Summer 1999): 305–12.

Gundy, Jeff. Review of *Spirit and Nature. Georgia Review* 47, no. 1 (Spring 1993): 180–83.

Havlik, R. J. Review of *American Nature Writers. Choice* 34, no. 8 (April 1997): 1305.

Howell, Richard W. Review of *Following the Brush. Journal of Asian History* 29, no. 2 (Fall 1995): 206–7.

Johnson, Trebbe. "Curriculum Vitae: Middlebury College Professor John Elder Bridges Nature and Literature." *Amicus Journal* 18, no. 3 (Fall 1996): 11–13. Correction to "Curriculum Vitae." *Amicus Journal* 18, no. 4 (Winter 1997): 10.

Kelly, Maggie. Review of *Reading the Mountains of Home. Georgia Review* 53, no. 2 (Summer 1999): 393–94.

Klinkenborg, Verlyn. "The Audubon Canon." Review of *The Norton Book of Nature Writing. Audubon* 100, no. 6 (November/December 1998): 102.

———. Review of *Reading the Mountains of Home. Audubon* 100, no. 4 (July/August 1998): 119.

Knickerbocker, Brad. Review of *The Norton Book of Nature Writing. Christian Science Monitor* (December 20, 1990): 10.

Kronen, Steve. Review of *Following the Brush*. *Georgia Review* 48, no. 2 (Summer 1994): 401–2.

Labaree, Benjamin W. Review of *The Norton Book of Nature Writing*. *New England Quarterly* 64, no. 2 (June 1991): 314–16.

MacDonald, Margaret Read. Review of *Family of Earth and Sky*. *Booklinks* 9, no. 4 (March 2000): 31.

Miller, David. "Slices of Wildlife." Review of *The Norton Book of Nature Writing*. *Sewanee Review* 99, no. 2 (Spring 1991): 319–407.

Morlock, Eric. Review of *Spirit and Nature*. *Whole Earth Review*, no. 8 (Autumn 1993): 37.

Murphy, Patrick. *Farther Afield in the Study of Nature-Oriented Literature*. Charlottesville: University Press of Virginia, 2000.

Parini, Jay. "Local Color: Regionalism and Literary Studies." *Chronicle of Higher Education* 43, no. 19 (January 17, 1997): A60.

———. "The Greening of the Humanities." *New York Times Magazine* (October 29, 1995): 52–53.

Perrin, Noel. "A Meeting of the Twain." Review of *Following the Brush*. *Los Angeles Times Book Review* (February 28, 1993): 1.

Reigler, Susan. "Words about Nature Special to the Courier-Journal." Review of *The Norton Book of Nature Writing*. *Louisville (Ky.) Courier Journal* (October 6, 1990): 14A.

Review of *Reading the Mountains of Home*. *Science Books and Films* 34, no. 7 (October 1998): 201.

Review of *Reading the Mountains of Home*. *Washington Post Book World* (August 23, 1998): 13.

Review of *Family of Earth and Sky*. *Kirkus Reviews* 66, no. 4 (February 15, 1998): 239–40.

Review of *American Nature Writers*. *Booklist* 93, no. 17 (May 1, 1997): 1524.

Review of *Reading the Mountains of Home*. *Kirkus Reviews* 62, no. 11 (June 1, 1994): 719.

Review of *Spirit and Nature. Publishers Weekly* 239, no. 20 (April 27, 1992): 259.

Reynolds, Susan Salter. Review of *Family of Earth and Sky. Los Angeles Times Book Review* (January 22, 1995): 6.

Richie, Donald. "Outsiders In." Review of *Following the Brush. Far Eastern Economic Review* 157, no. 39 (September 29, 1994): 45–46.

Robinson, David. Review of *Imagining the Earth. American Literature* 58, no. 3 (October 1986): 475.

Sanborn, Margaret, and Maria Simson. "Travel." Review of *Following the Brush. Publishers Weekly* 241, no. 3 (January 17, 1994): 301–2.

Sayen, Jamie. *"Reading the Mountains of Home:* A Dialogue between Wilderness and Culture." *Wild Earth* 9, no. 1 (Spring 1999): 94–95.

Seaman, Donna. "Nature's Way." Review of *Family of Earth and Sky. Booklist* 90, no. 21 (July 1994): 1906–7.

Scott, Mikey. Review of *The Norton Book of Nature Writing. Library Journal* 115, no. 4 (March 1, 1990): 110.

Solomon, Charles. Review of *Following the Brush. Los Angeles Times Book Review* (March 6, 1994): 8.

"Stories on the Trail." *Middlebury College Magazine* 67, no. 4 (Autumn 1993): 27–32.

Stuttaford, Genevieve. Review of *Reading the Mountains of Home. Publishers Weekly* 245, no. 9 (March 2, 1998): 50.

———. Review of *Following the Brush. Publishers Weekly* 239, no. 52 (November 30, 1992): 44.

———. Review of *The Norton Book of Nature Writing. Publishers Weekly* 237, no. 8 (February 23, 1990): 212.

Strauss, David. Review of *Following the Brush. American Literary History* 8, no. 3 (Fall 1996): 582–96.

Tallmadge, John. Review of *Family of Earth and Sky. Orion* 14, no. 1 (Winter 1995): 62.

Ward, Elizabeth. "In Japan, Eastern Exposure." Review of *Following the Brush. Washington Post* (February 26, 1993): C2.

Watkins, T. H. "Assignment Rio: Reading for a Better Planet." *Washington Post Book World* (May 31, 1992): 8–9.

Winkler, Karen J. "A Diversity of Approaches to Ecocriticism." *Chronicle of Higher Education* 42, no. 48 (August 9, 1996): A14.

————. "Inventing a New Field: The Study of Literature about the Environment." *Chronicle of Higher Education* 42, no. 48 (August 9, 1996): 8+.

Zvirin, Stephanie. Review of *Family of Earth and Sky*. *Booklist* 90, no. 21 (July 1994): 1929.

ACKNOWLEDGMENTS FOR
"THE FROG RUN"

by John Elder

I would like to thank Scott Slovic and Emilie Buchwald sincerely for inviting me to contribute to Milkweed's *Credo* series. My understanding of the character and possibilities of life in Vermont has been greatly enhanced by conversations with the following friends: David Brynn, Jackie Tuxill, Steve Harper, Chris McGrory Klyza, Megan Camp, Jeff Roberts, Rolf Diamant, Nora Mitchell, Jim Northup, Tom Butler, Darby Bradley, Phil Huffman, David Donath, Virginia Farley, Sam Cutting Sr., and Lindsey Ketchel. Jefferson Hunter, John Tallmadge, Robert Finch, and Scott Russell Sanders continue to help me in so many ways, along this path of teaching and writing. My wife, Rita, and our children, Rachel, Matthew, and Caleb, are always at the heart of my sense of place.

WORKS CITED

p. 5   Henry David Thoreau, *Walden* (New York:
          Modern Library, 1950), 280.

p. 10   Robert Frost, "Something for Hope," in *The
          Poetry of Robert Frost,* ed. Edward Connery
          Lathem (New York: Holt, Rinehart and
          Winston, 1969), 375–76. Copyright © 1951
          by Robert Frost, © 1975 by Lesley Frost
          Ballantine, and © 1923, 1947, 1969 by
          Henry Holt and Company, LLC. Reprinted
          with permission from Henry Holt and
          Company, LLC.

p. 13   Frost, "Come In," in *The Poetry of Robert Frost,*
          334.

p. 23   A. R. Ammons, "Corsons Inlet," in *Corsons
          Inlet: A Book of Poems* (Ithaca, N.Y.: Cornell
          University Press, 1965), 7.

p. 26   Joseph Battell, quoted in Jim Northup,
          "Joseph Battell: Once and Future Wildlands
          Philanthropist," *Wild Earth* 9, no. 2 (Summer
          1999): 17.

p. 26   Battell, quoted in Northup, 19.

p. 27   Aldo Leopold, *A Sand County Almanac* (New York: Oxford University Press, 1952), 203.

pp. 28–29   Battell, *Ellen or Whisperings of an Old Pine* (Middlebury, Vt.: American Publishing Company, 1903).

p. 30   Leslie Marmon Silko, "Landscape, History, and the Pueblo Imagination," in *The Ecocriticism Reader: Landmarks in Literary Ecology,* ed. Cheryll Glotfelty and Harold Fromm (Athens: University of Georgia Press, 1996), 268.

p. 33   Wendell Berry, "Conserving Forest Communities," in *Another Turn of the Crank* (Washington, D.C.: Counterpoint, 1995), 41.

pp. 38–39   Psalm 23, KJV.

p. 39   Lynn White Jr., "The Historical Roots of Our Ecological Crisis," *Science* (March 10, 1976): 1203–6.

pp. 45–46   John Milton, *Paradise Lost,* ed. A. W. Verity (New York: Cambridge University Press, 1921), bk. 1, lines 192–208.

p. 47   Edmund Burke, *A Philosophical Enquiry into the Origin of Our Ideas of the Sublime and the Beautiful* (London: R. and J. Dodsley, 1757).

pp. 47–48   Milton, *Paradise Lost,* bk. 12, lines 469–78.

p. 48   John Muir, *The Mountains of California,* new and enl. ed. (New York: The Century Co., 1913), 5.

pp. 51–52   William Wordsworth, *The Prelude* (New York: Norton, 1979), bk. 6, lines 619–40.

pp. 53–54   Annie Dillard, *Pilgrim at Tinker Creek* (New York: Perennial Classics, 1999), 35–36.

p. 54   Scott Slovic, *Seeking Awareness in American Nature Writing* (Salt Lake City: University of Utah Press, 1992).

pp. 54–55   Ralph Waldo Emerson, *Nature,* in *Nature, Addresses, and Lectures* (Cambridge, Mass.: Belknap Press, 1979), 8–9.

p. 55   Scott Russell Sanders, *Hunting for Hope* (Boston: Beacon Press, 1998).

p. 56   Bashō, *The Narrow Road to the Deep North,* trans. Noboyuki Yuasa (Harmondsworth, England: Penguin Books, 1968), 97.

p. 57   Bashō, *Narrow Road,* 118.57

p. 57   Tu Fu, "Advent of Spring," Trans. John Elder.

p. 58   Gary Snyder, "For the Children," in *Turtle Island* (New York: New Directions, 1974), 86. Copyright © 1974 by Gary Snyder. Reprinted with permission from New Directions Publishing Corp.

p. 61   Leopold, *A Sand County Almanac,* 203.

p. 61   Thoreau, *Walden,* 81, 82.

p. 61   Mary Oliver, "Turtle," in *House of Light* (Boston: Beacon Press, 1990), 22. Copyright © 1990 by Mary Oliver. Reprinted with permission from Beacon Press, Boston.

p. 62   "Master Hakuin's Chant in Praise of Zazen," in *Chants,* trans. Rochester Zen Center (Rochester, N.Y.: Rochester Zen Center, 1990), 23. Copyright © 1990 by Rochester Zen Center.

Reprinted with permission from the Rochester
Zen Center, Rochester, N.Y.

p. 62   Bashō. Trans. John Elder.

p. 63   Bashō. Trans. John Elder.

p. 64   Frost, "Dust of Snow," in *The Poetry of Robert Frost,* ed. Edward Connery Lathem (New York: Holt, Rinehart and Winston, 1969), 221. Copyright © 1951 by Robert Frost, © 1975 by Lesley Frost Ballantine, and © 1923, 1947, 1969 by Henry Holt and Company, LLC. Reprinted with permission from Henry Holt and Company, LLC.

pp. 65–66 Frost, "Nothing Gold Can Stay," in *The Poetry of Robert Frost,* ed. Edward Connery Lathem (New York: Holt, Rinehart and Winston, 1969), 222–23. Copyright © 1951 by Robert Frost, © 1975 by Lesley Frost Ballantine, and © 1923, 1947, 1969 by Henry Holt and Company, LLC. Reprinted with permission from Henry Holt and Company, LLC.

p. 66   Virgil, *Aeneid,* bk. 1, line 462.

p. 66   Frost, "In Hardwood Groves," in *The Poetry of Robert Frost,* 25.

p. 69   Frost, "Directive," in *The Poetry of Robert Frost,* ed. Edward Connery Lathem (New York: Holt, Rinehart and Winston, 1969), 377. Copyright © 1951 by Robert Frost, © 1975 by Lesley Frost Ballantine, and © 1923, 1947, 1969 by Henry Holt and Company, LLC. Reprinted with permission from Henry Holt and Company, LLC.

p. 89   Wordsworth, "Lines Written a Few Miles above

Tintern Abbey," in *Lyrical Ballads* (London: Longman, 1992), 211–12.

p. 89   Virginia Woolf, *To the Lighthouse* (New York: Harvest, 1989), 192.

p. 91   Frost, "After Apple-Picking," in *The Poetry of Robert Frost*, 69.

p. 91   John Keats, "To Autumn," in *The Complete Poetry and Selected Prose of John Keats*, ed. Harold Edgar Briggs (New York: Modern Library, 1951), 383.

pp. 101, 102, 104   Laurie Lane-Zucker, letter to Scott Slovic, January 19, 2001.

p. 106   Jay Parini, "The Greening of the Humanities," *New York Times Magazine* (October 29, 1995): 52.

p. 106   John Elder, "Climbing the Crests," *ADE Bulletin*, no. 117 (Fall 1997): 27.

p. 107   Elder, "Climbing the Crests," 27.

p. 107   Snyder, "For the Children," 86.

p. 107   Elder, "Climbing the Crests," 28.

p. 108   Elder, "Climbing the Crests," 28.

pp. 109–10 Elder, "Climbing the Crests," 29.

p. 110   Elder, "Climbing the Crests," 29.

pp. 111–12 Elder, *Reading the Mountains of Home* (Cambridge: Harvard University Press, 1998), 4.

p. 112   Peter Matthiessen, *The Snow Leopard* (New York: Viking, 1978), 242.

p. 113   Elder, *Reading the Mountains of Home*, 168.

pp. 114–15 Elder, 174.

p. 115   Elder, 175.

p. 124   Elder, "Project Statement," application
            for Fulbright Senior Research Award,
            September–December 2000. Unpublished.

p. 125   Elder, *Following the Brush: An American
            Encounter with Classical Japanese Culture*
            (Boston: Beacon Press, 1993), 21.

p. 126   Elder, *Following the Brush,* 22.

SCOTT SLOVIC, founding president of the Association for the Study of Literature and Environment (ASLE), currently serves as editor of the journal *ISLE: Interdisciplinary Studies in Literature and Environment.* He is the author of *Seeking Awareness in American Nature Writing: Henry Thoreau, Annie Dillard, Edward Abbey, Wendell Berry, Barry Lopez* (University of Utah Press, 1992); his edited and coedited books include *Being in the World: An Environmental Reader for Writers* (Macmillan, 1993), *Reading the Earth: New Directions in the Study of Literature and the Environment* (University of Idaho Press, 1998), *Literature and the Environment: A Reader on Nature and Culture* (Addison Wesley Longman, 1999), and *Getting Over the Color Green: Contemporary Environmental Literature of the Southwest* (University of Arizona Press, 2001). He is currently professor of English at the University of Nevada, Reno, where he directed the Center for Environmental Arts and Humanities from 1995 to 2001.

THE CREDO SERIES

Brown Dog of the Yaak:
Rick Bass

Winter Creek
John Daniel

Writing the Sacred into the Real
Alison Hawthorne Deming

The Frog Run
John Elder

Taking Care
William Kittredge

An American Child Supreme
John Nichols

Walking the High Ridge
Robert Michael Pyle

The Dream of the Marsh Wren
Pattiann Rogers

The Country of Language
Scott Russell Sanders

Shaped by Wind and Water
Ann Haymond Zwinger

THE WORLD AS HOME, the nonfiction publishing program of Milkweed Editions, is dedicated to exploring our relationship to the natural world. Not espousing any particular environmentalist or political agenda, these books are a forum for distinctive literary writing that not only alerts the reader to vital issues but offers personal testimonies to living harmoniously with other species in urban, rural, and wilderness communities.

MILKWEED EDITONS publishes with the intention of making a humane impact on society, in the belief that literature is a transformative art uniquely able to convey the essential experiences of the human heart and spirit. To that end, Milkweed publishes distinctive voices of literary merit in handsomely designed, visually dynamic books, exploring the ethical, cultural, and esthetic issues that free societies need continually to address. Milkweed Editions is a not-for-profit press.

JOIN US

Milkweed publishes adult and children's fiction, poetry, and, in its World As Home program, literary nonfiction about the natural world. Milkweed also hosts two websites: www.milkweed.org, where readers can find in-depth information about Milkweed books, authors, and programs, and www.worldashome.org, which is your online resource of books, organizations, and writings that explore ethical, esthetic, and cultural dimensions of our relationship to the natural world.

Since its genesis as *Milkweed Chronicle* in 1979, Milkweed has helped hundreds of emerging writers reach their readers. Thanks to the generosity of founda-tions and of individuals like you, Milkweed Editions is able to continue its nonprofit mission of publishing books chosen on the basis of literary merit—of how they impact the human heart and spirit—rather than on how they impact the bottom line. That's a miracle that our readers have made possible.

In addition to purchasing Milkweed books, you can join the growing community of Milkweed supporters. Individual contributions of any amount are both mean-ingful and welcome. Contact us for a Milkweed catalog or log on to www.milkweed.org and click on "About Milkweed," then "Why Join Milkweed," to find out about our donor program, or simply call (800) 520–6455 and ask about becoming one of Milkweed's contribu-tors. As a nonprofit press, Milkweed belongs to you, the community. Milkweed's board, its staff, and especially the authors whose careers you help launch thank you for reading our books and supporting our mission in any way you can.

Typeset in Stone Serif
by Stanton Publication Services, Inc.
Printed on acid-free, recycled
55# Frasier Miami Book Natural paper
by Friesen Corporation.